The

# GENEROSITY

Movement

## Activating Your Giving
## Like Never Before

ZACH MUELLER

WESTBOW
PRESS®
A DIVISION OF THOMAS NELSON
& ZONDERVAN

Scripture taken from the Holy Bible, NEW INTERNATIONAL VERSION®. Copyright © 1973, 1978, 1984, 2011 by Biblica, Inc. All rights reserved worldwide. Used by permission. NEW INTERNATIONAL VERSION® and NIV® are registered trademarks of Biblica, Inc. Use of either trademark for the offering of goods or services requires the prior written consent of Biblica US, Inc.

Scripture quotations are from The Holy Bible, English Standard Version® (ESV®), copyright © 2001 by Crossway, a publishing ministry of Good News Publishers. Used by permission. All rights reserved.

WestBow Press books may be ordered through booksellers or by contacting:

WestBow Press
A Division of Thomas Nelson & Zondervan
1663 Liberty Drive
Bloomington, IN 47403
www.westbowpress.com
1 (866) 928-1240

Because of the dynamic nature of the Internet, any web addresses or links contained in this book may have changed since publication and may no longer be valid. The views expressed in this work are solely those of the author and do not necessarily reflect the views of the publisher, and the publisher hereby disclaims any responsibility for them.

Any people depicted in stock imagery provided by Thinkstock are models, and such images are being used for illustrative purposes only. Certain stock imagery © Thinkstock.

ISBN: 978-1-5127-5527-5 (sc)
ISBN: 978-1-5127-5529-9 (hc)
ISBN: 978-1-5127-5528-2 (e)

Library of Congress Control Number: 2016914318

Print information available on the last page.

WestBow Press rev. date: 9/8/2016

# The Movement of Generosity in my Life

Above all else, thank you, God, for allowing me to be used by You and forever changing my life.

**Grandma**
You are the most generous person I have ever known. Grandma, thank you for teaching me, through your own life, what true generosity looks like; for pouring countless hours of your own time, talent, and treasure into my life and always encouraging and challenging me to do the same for others; for your constant prayers and awareness of our entire family; and for making each of us feel special in our own way. There's no doubt that your legacy lives on in the hearts of so many people. Fight the good fight of faith!

**Mom**
Thank you for the many conversations and continual love, care, and support. There is more to thank you for than I could write in the pages of this book. Thank you for continually implanting Philippians 4:13 into my life.

**Rachel**
We have definitely been through quite a bit together, smalls! Thank you for being my little sister and always knowing how to make me laugh and have a greater appreciation for life.

**Aunt Laurie**

You are the one who made it possible for me to go to college. Thank you for all your hospitality and for opening up your house in the summers when I was off from college so that I didn't have to drive as far to my internships.

**Susan**

You may not be my aunt through blood, but there is no doubt you have acted like an aunt and are considered one. Thank you for all your pep talks, humor, and honesty even when it would have been easier not to tell the truth. You always taught me, from a young age, how to be in the Lord's army.

**Rachel**

Ever since I met you, you have loved me for my weird quirks, let me talk out my frustrations on certain things, and supported my wildest dreams. You have laughed at jokes that were not all that funny and even cut my hair. I owe so much to you; thank you for being a model of what a Godly woman looks like. I love you, and I'm excited for more of our journey together.

**Countless others**

Dad, Feng, and Linna; my incredible and generous church staff; my supportive and high-energy youth staff; students and anyone who has poured into my life. This book would not have been possible without your generosity.

# Contents

# Introduction

As I sit in this office chair right now, piecing together the chapters and content for this book, I'm twenty-six years old, and aside from the four years I spent in college, I have lived in the southern part of Wisconsin for my entire life This, of course, means I love cheese and probably should love beer, but I am a pastor, and the one sip of beer I had when I was eight years old kept me away from it.

Even though I am still relatively young, when I look back at my life, I see that somehow I have been miraculously blessed with incredibly generous people. I have received some great gifts at Christmastime (Nintendo 64 and Power Rangers Deluxe Megazord, I am talking to you!). Maybe this is true for you too. Maybe it was a raise at your job, where you have been working hard. Maybe it was the savings bonds you received for your birthdays (which didn't seem generous at the time because you couldn't spend them, but ten years later you realized the value). We all can get used to generosity.

Conversely, I also have had my fair share of run-ins with people who were less than generous. Maybe you have had that moment when someone cut you off when changing lanes and presented you with a "you're number one" hand gesture. Maybe you looked in the freezer and realized that someone had eaten your favorite pint of Ben & Jerry's, which you'd marked with your name. (Well, someone did save you the calories.) When generosity is lacking, often our patience is lacking as well.

We all very much enjoy being the recipients of generosity. I have many memorable moments due to another person's generosity toward me. But here's my point. I don't really remember the brand of chocolate milk stocked in my Grandma's fridge, but I do remember I could always find it there. I don't play with my Nintendo 64 much anymore or take apart and rebuild my Power Rangers Megazord in my spare time, but I know my parents gave me those gifts because they who wanted to bless me not only with stuff but also show me love and keep me cool. The difference-making power of their generosity was not in any product or price tag but in the purposefulness of the person giving the gift.

What I love about generosity is that it is for everyone. Whether you are a youth pastor, head volunteer at your church, superstar high school athlete, manager at a department store, or maybe someone in the bookstore who grabbed this book because the cover was cool, generosity is totally in you. If God decided to be generous toward everyone by sending His Son, then that means any one of us can and should be living generously. Acts 20:35 says, "In everything I did, I showed you that by this kind of hard work we must help the weak, remembering the words the Lord Jesus himself said: 'It is more blessed to give than to receive." I hope this book offers you the opportunity to have a few laughs and gain some ideas for how you can spread generosity in your community and the wider area in which you live in, as well as get insight and aha moments that push you to activate your personal generosity like never before.

## Questions to Get Started

- How would you honestly evaluate your level of generosity (Acts 20:35)?
- Recall a time when you were given something special. We all know the feelings we have when we receive something special, but what feelings do you suppose the person who gave you the gift had?

# The Problem
# with Generosity

# 1

## Stranded Generosity

### *We Can Be Unaware*

I have a confession to make: I have an uncanny ability to forget things. I can set down my keys and five seconds later be pacing the floor, trying to find them, and praying that the Lord providentially places them in my pocket. While I am talking on my iPhone, I can instantly panic and tell the person to whom I am speaking that I can't seem to find my phone. (This always makes for a funny and embarrassing moment. Those who are laughing right now can probably relate.) I also have a knack for driving my car with little gas left in it and getting stranded somewhere. And this is where my story begins.

One Sunday afternoon, after having just said the last round of good-byes to the wonderful people of Poplar Creek Church, I walked to the back parking lot to hop in my car and meet up with my family for our regular after-church lunch stop at Wendy's. We always had a great time—who can't have a great conversation over a Baconator? I had to make a stop at Target, which was a little way down a very busy road from Wendy's. I knew I was a little low on gas—I'd gotten the orange warning light—but it was two miles away. So I took it to the limit, thinking my having been to church on Sunday morning would save me from getting stranded. Well, as I pulled up to the intersection of the busy road—with Target in sight—my 1997 Honda CRV shut down.

Running out of gas is quite embarrassing. To the outside world, it screams one of two things: (1) I have no money; or (2) I don't plan very well. I was probably guilty of both. But what happened next taught me a lot about generosity. I was blocking one lane of traffic at the busy intersection and watched as car after car passed me. One of them was even a cop car, and a few were church people. They would honk to put my clumsiness on display, drive around me, and yell out their windows. I'm sure plenty laughed at my humanity. I counted 139 cars pass me by before a cop finally put on his lights and actually pushed my car through the intersection like in a game of Frogger. He helped me into a parking lot where I could cry, call my mom, and have gas put in my car.

I completely understand that proper preparation prevents poor performance, but I realized that Sunday that generosity doesn't begin as a giving problem as much as an awareness of being able to give. I could not have made my situation any more apparent, considering that I could not move. I had my hazard lights on, indicating I was stuck and helpless, yet the people that day who passed me chose the simple and time-conscious route of going around me. If I flipped the story, and I was the one who had the opportunity to help, would I have stopped? I honestly don't know. So often, our opportunity to be generous in any particular moment is dictated by our schedules, stomachs, and sense of convenience, among other things that keep us from fueling up (see what I did there?) on compassion and a sense of hope in the lives of the stranded and lost.

## Questions to Challenge

- What are some of the reasons you choose to stay stranded instead of fueling up for generosity?
- Can you remember the last time you were aware of someone's need? How did you respond?

## The Generosity Challenge

At the end of each chapter, I've included a "Generosity Challenge." I believe growth can be birthed from practical experience. In the challenge, you will be given two options for expressing generosity. I would encourage you to choose one of the two options. What better way is there to retain what is read than by responding?

- Coordinate a day for working with other volunteers on a fund-raiser. Donate all the proceeds to a church or charity.
- Provide coffee for retail workers during holiday shopping events, such as Thanksgiving or Black Friday.

# 2

## Working and Wish Lists

### *We Can Be Selfish*

About a year ago, as Christmas approached, my young-adults pastor asked what I wanted as a gift. I didn't have an idea what I wanted but was immediately introduced to the most incredible way to find out what someone might want—the Amazon wish list. Up until that point, I could think of maybe one or two things that I wanted that year, but Amazon and its wish list began to completely open up my world. I was hooked! I spent hours searching for random things to add to my wish list. I humbly confess that by the time I was finished, I had nearly ten full pages of stuff I wanted, and I just pointed everyone to the list.

As I reviewed my list, I did not think, *Oh, wow, this is something my mom would really appreciate,* and I certainly didn't think, *I wonder how people in other countries who are in need are doing and how I could help.* These often aren't thoughts that float around in our minds. Breaking the habit of being inherently selfish is a tough battle with human nature. Much of what happens on this earth today revolves around status and success. We think, *If I can just be a person of influence ...* or *If I can just get ahead in life ...* or *If I can have the biggest ministry ...* Our struggle, in our selfishness, is that it leads us to money or material possessions to make us feel like we have arrived. But Matthew 6:24 spells it out for us plainly: "No one can serve two masters. Either you will hate the one and love the other, or you will be devoted to the one and despise the other. You cannot serve both God and money" (NIV).

Before you close this book and write a bad review of it, understand what I am getting at. Many people in the secular world probably look at Matthew 6:24 and say they can't serve the Lord because they enjoy their things that make them happy. But that is far from it. Notice it says you can't *serve* two masters. It doesn't say you can't enjoy nice things. Remember that God believes in hard work and knows about it too. Even though He is God, He did create the world in six days and rested on the seventh, so He understands hard work! . I think He is more concerned with asking, "Is your priority found in Me?" Does this rule over your life so much that it keeps you from real blessings and real riches? What are you actively doing to make your generosity grow? What is the element in your life that hinders your humility?

As a pastor working with middle school and high school students, I know that if I were to tell a student who was unchurched to come to my Wednesday night service and hear about Jesus and His love for us, chances lean more toward me hearing a response that wouldn't excite me. Students who haven't been to my youth ministry don't jump with excitement at the word *church.* They do, however, jump at the chance to win an iWatch or a $500 gift card.

Instead of relying on God's riches, I have relied on earthly resources. For a stretch of time, I wanted to see our numbers grow, so we began to hold giveaways just about every other week. After a while, I noticed people collect their prizes and leave. I might have appeared generous, but my ministry did not grow. In trying to grow the ministry numerically, I had focused my attention on what someone could get, instead of what could be given to God to grow spiritually. Those were some of the most frustrating and expensive—yet educational—moments in my life so far. I think I was convinced that I could have access to someone's heart through material things, but it could only be found through the Savior.

Thank God that He always has a plan and a way out for anything we could do that goes against His plan. What people sometimes forget to notice is that God continues to show Himself selfless each and every day. Sure, we make a big deal about the cross—and rightfully so—but what about the breath you take each day? God's there for it. The hairs on your head? He records them. Your big moments? He rejoices. Your sad moments? He mourns. I think God knows selfishness is not an easy discipline to break. That is why He puts His selflessness on display each day for us to see. He is a Creator who owns the universe yet chooses to share it.

Remember that you were made in His image, the most selfless being. Because of that, your Master is the only one who has enough access to your heart to make you feel less that you are striving and more that you are arriving.

## Questions to Challenge

- What do you allow in your life today that enhances your habit of selfishness?
- How has your selfishness changed your heart?

**The Generosity Challenge**

- Plan a small get-together dedicated to honoring someone who has been helpful to the community and people around him or her.
- Spend a few hours cleaning up a local park.

# 3

## The Doubting Disciple

### *Fear over Faith and Trust*

Having been around a little while, even though I mentioned it's been only twenty-six years and I'm still a kid at heart, I like to think that that I have faith in myself and that I can both trust and be trusted. That was not always the case, however, and maybe you can relate.

Some kids are wired to believe anything they hear. They're the type of kids who will believe someone's telling them they can fly. That's probably just being gullible. Then there are the kids who can't seem to believe much of anything. They won't believe someone owns something unless that something is in the person's hand. I relate very well to this type of kid.

When I was between the ages of four and twelve, I was a little pessimistic. If someone could told me he could do something cool or got a sweet new bike, my response was two words: "Prove it."

One time I had a friend over who told me he had a pocket knife. I was not allowed to have a pocket knife, so I was certain there was no way he could possibly have one. I told him to prove it. He went back to his house, grabbed his shiny Swiss army blade, and came back to show it to me. I was in total shock and awe but also uncomfortable, considering it was a weapon. For some reason I remember that day vividly and the fact that I was proven wrong by my friend. Over the course of my "prove it" years, I lost quite a few challenges and realized honesty does exist in people. I also won a few challenges when the people I asked to "prove it" couldn't do so, leaving friends feeling awkward and caught.

What did I really accomplish during this "prove it" phase? When I was right, the person who was caught in a lie probably thought twice before making the same claim again. Most of the time, however, I wasn't right, and it left that person second-guessing if he ever wanted to tell me anything and if I could be trusted. Honestly, I think I still have some "prove it" mentality, and I often challenge the one person I love the most.

In John 20:24–29, we come across a man who is the total "prove it" package. His name is Thomas, the doubting disciple. Shortly, after Jesus resurrected, the disciples discovered that He had risen as He said He would; they were all convinced. Seeing Jesus alive and hearing His voice was reason enough for them to have faith and trust that it was Him. I'm not exactly sure where Thomas was in all this, but he clearly had other plans or maybe was asking someone else to "prove it." The disciples came back and told Thomas what they'd seen and tried to convince Thomas–a man who had been in their life group for a long time— that Jesus was back. Thomas responded with a "prove it" kind of statement:

"But he said to them, 'Unless I see in his hands the mark of the nails, and place my finger into the mark of the nails, and place my hand into his side, I will never believe'" (John 20:25 NIV).

Heavy words from a guy who just three days earlier was most likely a witness to the crucifixion of Jesus. Not only that but as a disciple of Jesus, he witnessed many miracles that Jesus

Himself performed, yet he was not convinced by the ones closest to him, who were family. He went so far as to say he would *never* believe. A lot like Thomas was skeptical about Jesus's rising from the dead, we often have that same mentality in regard to generosity. We get into places and spaces where we ask God to show us generosity, and then when it does not happen, we become fearful that He may have forgotten about us or that we aren't in His best interest. What we tend to forget, though—and just as Thomas mentioned—there were marks in Jesus's hands from the nails and a wound from the spear that was put in His side. We are convinced of what has happened, but we still gather reasons to be even more convinced. The question I have had to ask in my own life is this:

"What more does God need to do to convince me of Him?"

If I live my entire life needing to continually be convinced of a man who has already given all of Himself to me, I may never find myself convinced. I think this is what brings a separation for people in their relationships with God, more so than we understand. God is more concerned with matters of the heart, so when He gives, it is meant to make a connection to the heart. He gives in ways that show we can trust and have faith in Him, that His generosity toward us always points to us believing in Him, and that we have an opportunity to be generous to others.

The story of Thomas the Doubter doesn't end here, because Jesus generosity pushes us out of fear and into faith and trust. On the eighth day, the disciples again were having a little hangouthanging out, probably enjoying some Chick-Fil-A and catching up on the latest happenings. I am sure they didn't count the days since their previous conversation with Thomas, but the number eight has significance because in scriptural terms, it means "new beginnings" or "being born again." Thomas, as a disciple and close friend of Jesus, was about to have a new beginning.

Although the doors were locked, Jesus came and stood among them and said, "Peace be with you."

"Then he said to Thomas, 'Put your finger here, and see my hands; and put out your hand, and place it in my side. Do not disbelieve, but believe.' Thomas answered him, 'My Lord and my God!' Jesus said to him, 'Have you believed because you have seen me?'" (John 20:27–29 NIV).

I love that first part. As if rising from the dead was not convincing enough that Jesus was alive and the Savior of the world, before He even shows Thomas His hands and sides, He appears, in spite of a locked door. Fear often is the locked door of our lives that holds God in a place of needing to generously prove Himself, yet effortlessly, He can open the door. Jesus obviously was aware that Thomas could very well be paranoid that an intruder was breaking into a house with locked doors. He says, "Peace be with you." I imagine that if this account makes it to the big screen someday, this could be an iconic line. Remember when I talked about awareness? Jesus is full of awareness and offers His peace but also speaks to Thomas's unbelief without having been in the room when Thomas made his "prove it" statement. Two times Jesus shows Himself as Jesus before He shows His hands and side. Is that generosity or what? It seems, though, that Thomas missed those moments because Thomas didn't act like he was convinced it was Jesus.

I hope I never become so complacent in my relationship with God that it takes two or three times for God to show me who He is. Fear can move our minds away from the moment of God's making Himself known. But thank God He redeems, even when we are not always on point.

Thomas then got a little bit of an active demonstration and anatomy lesson from Jesus. Have you ever worked on a project for a class? There often is a three-step process when a project is given: hear the teacher's instruction, research and do the work, and then see the results of your finished project. We can sometimes have an idea or see the project finished in our minds, but until we do the work, it stays in our minds. Jesus gave the instruction to Thomas and then followed with an action. Psalm 34:8 says, "Taste and see that the LORD is good; blessed is the one who takes refuge in him" (NIV). Jesus gives this doubter, who is most likely fearful, an action to perform, and Thomas trusts Jesus just enough to put his fingers in the marks of Jesus's hands and side.

At that moment, everything began to change, as he acknowledges the proof that he saw, spiritually and physically, and a new beginning happened.

Our generosity can model Jesus in such a way that new beginnings can happen for people. We might not be able to put unbelievers' fingers into the hands of Jesus, but we can offer them a generous hand. We may not be able to put unbelievers' hands into the side of Jesus, but we can walk by their sides as they live moments in their lives. At the moment of Thomas's new beginning, I believe there was a resurgence of generosity that stirred in his heart to point people to faith and trust in Jesus. Like a school project, I can have Jesus's generosity backward sometimes. I want to see what He will do—the finished project— and then make a decision on whether it's worth it to be generous and serve Him with my time, talent, and treasure. The problem with that is that the work He did in His death and resurrection has been finished, and newfound faith can flow from that place. I may not be able to see Him physically, but my faith should rest in His completed work on the cross.

I have two more quick points about Thomas. Jesus finished the moment with Thomas and the disciples by saying this:

"Blessed are those who have not seen and yet have believed" (John 20:29 NIV).

Blessed. I don't know about you, but someone who opens closed doors and comes with peace is someone from whom I want to receive a blessing. What if everyone came to the conclusion that we could choose to live in godly generosity because we believe in God's blessing? I tend to be a visual person. God says He will bless those who have not seen but believe, but it is not always particularly easy because His blessing involves faith and trust, while being free of fear. I don't think He's saying that Thomas could not be blessed because he doubted, but Thomas missed out on the blessing God would give to the one who has not seen but still believes. This is us, right? We have not physically seen God, yet we believe Him to be who He says He is. Immediately after, it is confirmed to us in John 20:30–31.

"Now Jesus did many other signs in the presence of the disciples, which are not written in this book; but these are written so that you may believe that Jesus is the Christ, the Son of God, and that by believing you may have life in his name" (NIV).

The purpose of the book of John, Jesus's life of generosity, is right here; we read His word, see His goodness, and believe. And then we have life in His name, the name that is full of trust and faith and is exempt from fear.

## Questions to Challenge

- How has God been faithful in your life? Are you convinced of God's generosity in your life?
- What part of generosity leaves you the most fearful? What would it take to break that fear?

## The Generosity Challenge

- Ask people to write encouraging note cards that can be placed in an album and given to someone who is medically ill.
- Pass out cold bottled water during a community event in the summertime (e.g., Fourth of July, National Night Out).

# 4

## Convicting Chore Charts

### *I Will Be Generous but under One Condition.*

When I was a kid, I had an incredible responsibility that I loved and appreciated called chores. Maybe you can sense some sarcasm in that, but to this day, I do my own laundry and fold it sometimes. As a kid, I remember having multiple charts, incentives, tickets—really just anything to get me to do my chores. I remember many moments when I dreaded going outside to mow the lawn or, even worse, shovel snow from the driveway (this seemed to happen more often because I grew up in Wisconsin). In the particular moment, these chores were not how I wanted to spend my time, but I remember feeling motivated by one thought: at the end of the week, I would receive my reward, depending on the current operating system my parents had put in place. Usually, each chore was rated and priced according to level of difficulty, but I could usually make between seven and ten dollars.

At some point in our lives, we upgraded from the money that we got for doing our chores at home to getting a job, often making minimum wage. After ten or twenty hours of work each week (depending on if we were in school), every two weeks we would receive a paycheck.

It might be difficult today to find any kids who really enjoy all their chores. There may be one or—rarely—two chores that they like to do, or maybe it's because they can do the chore quickly and can get it out of the way, but for the most part, they don't like these responsibilities. I am not a parent yet, but as a kid I remember that I was driven to get up early or to take out smelly trash by the condition that I would get that hard-earned money only if I did my chores. And I spent my money generously on myself at the sports card shop down the road.

We are a culture that is driven by incentives and conditions. Friends-and-family discounts, customer appreciation, "buy one; get one free," and throw-ins are all music to our ears. I usually will make decisions based on who is giving me the best deal for the least amount of work or cost to me.

When it comes to our spiritual lives, many of us try to live (and choose) that same way. We expect God's greatest riches and incentives, while putting in the least amount of work possible. We want God to make our families prosper, give us consistent jobs, and provide us with great friends and a rockin' spiritual life, all for the low cost of our waking up on Sunday morning to get to church. When we don't get these things, we then become confused as to why God doesn't seem to be generous to us.

We tend to miss critical moments—where we can help the person on the side of the road or give a meal to the homeless person—because we live under the contract of condition. When was the last time you offered your help and service to someone without an expectation or even a thought of return? This could be a good question for us to ask ourselves, but how about this additional question:

*When was the last time you made the decision to help someone because you remembered there's a reward waiting for you in heaven?*

Jesus was undeniably the most generous person to grace this earth, and, yes, He was and still is perfect, but what was His motive? Was it to put extra money in His pocket? Was it to get people to believe in Him? Some might say yes, but remember that He healed lepers who never thanked Him. The priority was always what they could receive, and their believing was seen as a bonus. I think His motivation was to point people back to His Father God, who was the reward these people were waiting for, though they didn't realize they had a need to meet Him. It just so happened to be the reward Jesus was waiting for—to be with His dad in heaven again.

I believe that God does not work on a system that says, "What you give determines what you will get." God gave everything He had and put it all out there when He sent His Son to a cross for our lives. Once that transaction was completed, however, we had—and now have—the opportunity to be receivers of God's fullness and generosity. Our opportunity to become generous is enhanced when we understand that. I do not particularly work hard to serve God and honor Him with my life, based on *what* He did but because of *who* He is—that He would make a decision to sacrifice something for me, knowing I may not always sacrifice for Him. That's why I want to be a generous person, not a person who *can be* generous.

Regardless of how much time, talent, or treasure we put in our jobs, families, and friends, we will never be able to live up to what God gives. If God ever were to give us conditions to His love and grace, we would always come up short. By His being unconditional, though, we have access to the heart and characteristics of God.

The greatest moments of shock in my parents' lives were the times when I did chores around the house without expectation or allowance being given to me. I believe the best and easiest way we point people to Jesus is generosity without strings attached. His generosity is unconditional, and because of that I want to be someone who is unconditional in the way I treat others and who encourages others to do the same.

## Questions to Challenge

- When was the last time you were generous without any incentive?
- How do conditions slow down your desire to be generous?

## The Generosity Challenge

- Offer to pay for the meal of the person behind you in the drive-through.
- Take care of someone's bus ticket or parking-meter money.

# 5

## You Got This, Bro

### *We Are Selective*

I may not be the type of person who hits the gym or likes to wrestle or surf, but I do see myself as a "bro" by nature. I enjoy watching football games or playing a round of Madden on my Xbox from time to time. I found that when I am a part of these activities and hanging around my guy friends, the word "bro" gets thrown around pretty often. (I sometimes even say it like wrestling superstar Hulk Hogan.) I also found that I enjoy being encouraging, especially for things that I particularly don't want to do, and from there we have the term, "You got this, bro."

Anyone reading this book is not allowed to pass judgment on it because ... well, that's God's job. I may hear about it when I see Him someday, but I can be a "you got this, bro" kind of guy. This phrase usually is code for one of two things:

1. I really don't want to do this, so I am passing it off to you.
2. I'm so glad I'm not in your position. It seems impossible, but good luck with that!

Do you know what I am referencing now? I know I am horrible at anything that has to do with organization, and I don't particularly enjoy organizing, so I find someone else to do it and say, "Hey, you got this, bro!" Or maybe it was back in high school, when a guy is ready to ask a girl to prom. You know his chances are pretty slim, but you say, "Hey, you got this, bro!" because you're glad you will not be the recipient of that rejection. Generosity can bring the best out of "you got this, bro." Some call it encouragement; I call it escape.

How many people do you know who have been affected because of your "you got this, bro" mentality when it comes to your generosity? Human nature can cause us to be selective in whom we influence (or how we influence), and when we become selective, we have an expectation that someone else can very well take care of it. David has a pretty good example of what can happen when you decide to say "no more" to leaving it to another bro.

First Samuel 17 focuses on a moment for which David will be forever known. David, as we all know from our *Veggie Tales* and flannel-graph days, is a boy who probably was somewhat small in stature and possibly had a high voice. He was the youngest of Jesse's eight sons. David had three older brothers who were engaged in a battle, and he was elected to be the delivery boy for the army, bringing the bread and cheese. David did his part, being generous by helping to take care of the needs of those involved in battle, but that did not last very long. One morning, David left his sheep behind and brought his brothers their lunch. He got their lunch to them just in time for Goliath's show. Goliath was a beast of a man; he was referred to as a champion, which meant this was not his first battle. (I feel sorry for the other guy.) Here are just some of his stats:

> And there came out from the camp of the Philistines a champion named Goliath of Gath, whose height was six cubits and a span. He had a helmet of bronze on his head, and he was armed with a coat of mail, and the weight of the coat was five thousand shekels of bronze. And he had bronze armor on his legs, and a javelin of bronze slung between his shoulders. The shaft of his spear was like a weaver's beam, and his spear's head weighed six hundred shekels of iron. And his shield-bearer went before him. (1 Samuel 17:4–7 NIV)

Just to give you a little idea of who David was about to battle, Goliath was about nine foot six. He wore a breastplate that weighed 125 pounds, and the blade of his spear—the blade!—weighed fifteen pounds. (This guy was like the kid in middle school who already has armpit hair, a full-grown beard, and looks like he should be someone's uncle.) Scripture says that Goliath taunted the Israelites, and it makes sense if he looked like that. Goliath could have wiped out an entire army, most likely on his own, but he chose to put his power on display and bring the Israelites into what they knew would be a losing battle.

The Israelite army, sometimes like our opportunities to be generous, took one look at this giant and immediately ran in the other direction. I feel like sometimes I can be the Israelite army. When it comes to generosity, I can seem to generously enjoy generously encouraging other people to take care of what God has asked me to do. I'm not usually a fan of people who like to play the worst-case-scenario game, but what would happen if every person lived a life that took a pass on generosity? I can only imagine the conversation these guys were having as they sat in their camps, pointing at each other and volunteering someone else to basically be torn apart by Goliath. How scared were these guys, and how much did they volunteer each other for this battle?

> And the men of Israel said, "Have you seen this man who has come up? Surely he has come up to defy Israel. And the king will enrich the man who kills him with great riches and will give him his daughter and make his father's house free in Israel." And David said to the men who stood by him, "What shall be done for the man who kills this Philistine and takes away the reproach from Israel? For who is this uncircumcised Philistine, that he should defy the armies of the living God?" And the people answered him in the same way, "So shall it be done to the man who kills him." (NIV)

Not even great riches or the king's cute daughter could convince these men to battle this giant. They received the most stunning and, at the same time, most relieving news possible when David told Saul that he would fight the Philistine, Goliath. David didn't make excuses why he should not be the one; he gave reasons why he should be.

> And David said to Saul, "Let no man's heart fail because of him. Your servant will go and fight with this Philistine." And Saul said to David, "You are not able to go against this Philistine to fight with him, for you are but a youth, and he has been a man of war from his youth." [34] But David said to Saul, "Your servant used to keep sheep for his father. And when there came a lion, or a bear, and took a lamb from the flock, I went after him and struck him and delivered it out of his mouth. And if he arose against me, I caught him by his beard

and struck him and killed him. Your servant has struck down both lions and bears, and this uncircumcised Philistine shall be like one of them, for he has defied the armies of the living God." And David said, "The LORD who delivered me from the paw of the lion and from the paw of the bear will deliver me from the hand of this Philistine." (NIV)

I look at this and think, *How often am I looking for reasons to be generous, no matter what giant stands in my way of completing that?* Or do I allow myself to lose to the giants of schedules, meetings, food, friends, Netflix, or anything else that keeps me from being victorious. Do I notice what God has done in my life and then allow that to motivate me to feel like I can be generous to anyone and in any circumstance? Do I choose to deliver when I am aware of someone's need and then give thanks to my deliverer for the chance to do so?

Saul speculated a little bit by saying David was too young, but then he said and acted in a "you got this, bro" kind of way. He first said, "Go, and the Lord be with you!" I can appreciate his inclusion of the Lord, but his vote of confidence feels like defeating Goliath is impossible. He then loaded up David with unfit armor, so David decided to go without. The account ends with David hurling a stone at Goliath and then cutting off his head. One of the final things mentioned in that section of scripture is that the Israelites plundered the camp of the Philistines.

Many can win through one person's decision to be generous. I love how it mentions that the people of Israel plundered the camp. They may not have slayed the giant, but they were rewarded because of his death. In all of this, though, the greatest reward went to David, the one who did not let an opportunity pass him by, no matter how big it seemed or how many people said, "You got this, bro." He was only supposed to drop off a couple of things for his brother, but he took the opportunity to be generous to his Israelite people, he became a hero of the faith. The entire time, David knew this would not be at all possible without God on his side, fighting for him.

Jesus so desperately wants to be involved in our efforts to be generous. That is why when it comes to generosity, the term "you got this, bro" really is nonexistent. Some of the moments when I have felt God's presence the most are when I am in the process of or have just finished being generous toward someone. Jesus takes our "you got this, bro" and turns it into "we got this, bro." Really, what movements of generosity can fail when you have the most generous being on your side?

## Questions to Challenge

- What do you believe is the difference between selection and passion?
- What kind of effect does partnering with someone in generosity have on both your lives?

## The Generosity Challenge

- Get a bunch of people to fill someone's Facebook wall with compliments and specific things you appreciate about that person.
- Offer to drop off a meal to the parent in a single-parent home.

# 6

## A Quick Pick-Me-Up

Addressing truth can sometimes be one of the most difficult things because it makes us aware that we are flawed people. You might wonder, *Why in the world would I buy a book that is going to expose all the things I should not be?* My prayer for you is that you will be encouraged and excited about giving your generosity to this desperate world. Showing what generosity is not should help you to see what, why, and how you can and should be generous.

We all have generosity in us; it's just a matter of whether we allow our generosity to be active in our lives. Some people may feel they are too far gone to ever be generous. Maybe you have read the last couple of chapters and feel defeated because you identify strongly with all of the traits that generosity is *not*. I want to encourage you, though, that each person identifies in some form of what he or she is not; that, unfortunately, is a part of human nature. We like what we like when we like it and how we like it! (What a tongue-twister!) God never said this life was going to be easy, but He did say that He would be a part of our lives every step of the way. So keep reading and keep growing because good leaders are good readers!

## Questions to Challenge

- Which area in the previous section do you most identify with? Why?
- What do you believe will help you to move out of the area with which you most identify?

# Aware
# Intentional
# Sacrificial
# Available

# 7

## Roller Coasters and Big Words

When I was growing up, I was never a big fan of heights. I'm not sure what, exactly, left me feeling this way, but I knew I did not like the sensation of going off a big drop and having my stomach in my chest, I was a big fan, however, of the ground and having my feet on it. I remember one summer when I was ten years old, my relatives and my family took a trip to Six Flags Great America in Illinois for a day full of thrill rides. For me, it was a day of complete horror and trembling. For most of the day, I was able to avoid all roller coasters and big rides—until we arrived in the kids' section. I gladly rode all the rides in that kids' section without any problem—and then I noticed a small roller coaster out of the corner of my eye. Hoping no one else would see it, I carried on until one of my four-year-old cousins spotted it and asked if we could all ride it. I just could not stand the fact that my cousins, who were less than half my age, would go on this ride when I would not, so I thought, *How bad could it be?*

I know it was not the scariest ride in the park by any means, but the next thing that happened for my terrified ten-year-old self surprised me. I held my mom's hand as we went over every three-foot hill, while my four-year-old cousins had their hands raised in the air the entire time. Once I got off the ride, though, a sense of bravery came over me that made me feel like I'd conquered the world. Ever since that day, I have grown to like roller coasters and can manage them without holding my mom's hand.

Before that day on the roller coaster, you would have thought that I would live the rest of my life without going on a roller coaster, but once I got over that small hill and realized my victory and how good it felt, I wanted to keep going. This is kind of how I imagine generosity is sometimes. People have different areas in which they passionately invest their generosity. Whether it's for homeless people, orphans, the abused, or many others, they found those areas because they took hold of a moment to be generous, and they now are forever passionate about. If you look at the life of Jesus, you'll realize His life was a little bit of a roller coaster. He preached on the tops of mountains and healed people who were in valleys. He touched the life of a crippled man by a pool and resisted temptation in the desert. Jesus experienced different turns and curves and still managed to live with incredible generosity. I find it becomes difficult sometimes to live generously when I can't feel generous about myself. When I am high, my generosity is high, and when I am low, my generosity is low.

Living generously is not always easy; actually, it rarely is. If we open ourselves up to being generous, chances are it will stop us in the middle of what we are doing, make us go out of our way, pull us from what we enjoy, and not always give us back something tangible. The words associated with generosity in an earthly sense are not usually prosperity, popularity, and possibilities. I think this is what God means in Romans 12:2 when it says,

"Do not conform to the pattern of this world, but be transformed by the renewing of your mind. Then you will be able to test and approve what God's will is—his good, pleasing and perfect will" (NIV).

If we are truly living a life of opening ourselves up to being generous, we receive more than we could ever ask for—more than a thank-you text or a card.

In these next chapters, you will see words that describe generosity. Remember that it is cool to receive accolades and love from people, to be honored and loved for what you have done, but these things pale in comparison to what these words will mean from God in heaven. That we have the opportunity live out an earthly mission for an eternal cause.

Generosity is *aware.*

a·ware (/əˈwer/), *adjective*

having knowledge or perception of a situation or fact

# 8

## Seeing and Slowing Down

I wear contact lenses. Before I had contact lenses, I had glasses. My eyesight isn't terrible, but I have needed some type of corrective lenses for most of my life. Eye problems run in my family; my mom, dad, and sister all wear glasses. With my glasses or contacts, I can see things without any problem, but if I do not have either of those, I can look down and my feet are blurry. Vision can be taken for granted until you realize you can't see well.

"Seeing" generosity can often feel like a day without glasses or contacts. You want to be generous and help people and live out God's will for your life that day, but before you know it, you begin to question where in the world twenty-four hours possibly could have gone. You watch a little ESPN, you put the kids to bed, maybe have a bowl of ice cream, and pray that tomorrow you can do better. Being generous is great because you can plan generosity, but it can also sneak up on you and show up randomly in the form of someone needing assistance. Whatever the case may be, in order to meet the need, you must be able to see the need. To get an idea of what awareness to living generously look likes, consider the following two sisters:

Jesus and His disciples rolled into the village, where a woman named Martha invited them into her house. I don't know if you have ever hosted a large family gathering, but my family spends tons of time preparing by cleaning the house, arranging food, and making sure things look good. Now, imagine Martha is getting ready to invite not only Jesus but up to twelve hungry men who have been traveling with Him. We get a pretty good vibe that she is trying to get everything ready. She is moving fast and serving up a storm. Then we have Martha's sister, Mary, who up to that point was probably racing around, getting the house ready, so Jesus and His disciples felt welcome. Something happened once Jesus came in the house, though, that made Martha stop dead in her tracks.

"And she had a sister called Mary, who sat at the Lord's feet and listened to his teaching" (Luke 10:39 NIV).

In the midst of probably the most chaotic moment, welcoming all these people and inviting them in, Mary slowed everything down and decided to just sit on the floor—not exactly the first idea we have when people come to our homes. While it is strange that Mary did this, we can see it as a dynamic statement of what it means to be aware of generosity. When Jesus taught, it wasn't too difficult to lock on the words He spoke. The posture of sitting shows that Mary was not planning on moving any time soon. Mary was in the moment and saw the need to listen to Jesus and His teachings. She was drawn into a relational moment and was aware that this was of high significance. At the same time, Martha went on the defensive about her sister's actions and called Jesus into question about it

"But Martha was distracted with much serving. And she went up to him and said, "Lord, do you not care that my sister has left me to serve alone? Tell her then to help me" (Luke 10:40 NIV).

Martha was justified in what she said; in that time, it was proper for the ladies to serve and help in being hospitable. She probably stopped Jesus in the middle of His teaching, and Jesus responded.

"But the Lord answered her, "Martha, Martha, you are anxious and troubled about many things, but one thing is necessary. Mary has chosen the good portion, which will not be taken away from her" (Luke 10:41-42 NIV).

Here, Jesus said Martha's name not once but twice. Jesus noticed how occupied she was, and while she was doing a good thing, she was missing the main thing because she was moving too fast. We often live like this, moving vicariously through life. Generosity that could have existed is missed. Mary sat at Jesus's feet because she didn't want to be distracted even a little. She gave all her attention to God and was aware that her time was worth giving. A lot of great opportunities impact our world. Sometimes we get so "in the moment" to move and serve that we don't slow down enough to realize that the generosity should have pointed to our Savior. Are we more concerned about doing something good, instead of doing something God? Have we slowed down enough to understand and be aware of the needs around us? To truly have generosity ring loudly in our lives, it must revolve around what is necessary—and that is having our eyes set on Jesus. If we do that we will not rob ourselves of a lifestyle of generosity.

## Questions to Encourage

- Of what area of generosity are you the most aware? What led you to that area?
- Share about a time when someone took notice of your generosity. What feeling did that leave you with?

**The Generosity Challenge**

- Handwrite a note of encouragement to let a friend know that you are thinking of and praying for him or her. (You might be surprised at what something so simple can do for someone.)
- Keep track of special dates and spend time thanking the ones for whom that day was made (e.g., Administrative Assistants Day, Educators Appreciation Day).

Generosity is *intentional.*

in·ten·tion·al (in'ten(t)SH(ə)n(ə)l), *adjective*

done on purpose; deliberate

# 9

## A Priest, a Levite, and a Samaritan

Have you ever (and maybe still do) spent time building a snow fort? One winter during my Christmas break from school, I remember running outside where there was a giant mound of snow just beyond the fence in a business parking lot. I usually woke up around nine in the morning, watched some Nickelodeon, ate some Rice Krispies cereal, and then headed out to the mound of snow to start my digging. My friends and I spent countless hours, almost like it was our full-time job, digging and shoveling out tunnels for our snow fort. After about a forty-hour workweek, we finally connected the tunnels that were on opposite sides of this massive pile of snow. We never got around to putting a TV or electrical in there, but we hung out in that fort for most of our break, until the next snowfall covered the tunnels. That was most likely the greatest fort I ever built.

Starting out, my friends and I did not know how this pile of snow would turn out, but we all could see the finished project and made a collaborative effort to get us to that place. In that, the process was in place. We went home each night after a long day of digging and held each other accountable to be there at ten or eleven the next morning, snow pants on and ready to go. The finished project was enjoyable because of the amount of time we put into it, but I believe, whether we knew it or not, it was more enjoyable because we were intentional about putting the time in and getting the fort finished. We were intentional in how to angle the tunnels just right so that they would connect. We were intentional about where we put certain rooms in the tunnel because we didn't want the upstairs to collapse into the downstairs. We were pretty smart and almost like mini-architects. We were intentional about helping each other because we knew without each other, building the fort would not be possible.

In order for us to have an intention, something needs to catch our attention. When we decide to clean house, the house being dirty or the fact that relatives are coming over to hang out is what catches our attention. Our calendar that reminds us of a meeting we have often catches our attention and so we get in the car and get to that meeting. Watching TV and seeing a commercial for a great new place to eat often catches our attention (and our stomachs' attention that we are hungry), so we go eat. We all have had something brought to our attention, but are we willing to go the extra step and act on our intention?

Luke 10:25–37 (NIV) gives us an incredible example of intentional generosity. Jesus told a lawyer, who was likely very highly educated, that in order to inherit eternal life, "you shall love the Lord your God with all your heart, soul, mind, and strength" and to "love your neighbor as yourself." Jesus really gave the key to what intentional generosity looks like. This lawyer, being the wise guy he is and having a thirst for justice, asked Jesus who His neighbor is and toward whom he was meant to be generous. See, this lawyer probably only gave attention to people who lived to the level of his status, so much so that Jesus gave a pretty blunt and extreme example to get this man's attention.

"Jesus replied, "A man was going down from Jerusalem to Jericho, and he fell among robbers, who stripped him and beat him and departed, leaving him half dead" (Luke 10:30 NIV).

Jesus paints the picture of a Levite, a man who is left with nothing, as being half dead—and oh, he is also naked. This man most likely would stick out to anyone passing by, at least a lot more than he did before he was robbed. But help is on the way, right? Wrong. First, we get a priest, a God-fearing and God-loving man, who does ministry for a living and has been called to people. We would expect him to be intentional or to at least call an ambulance, but scripture says he sees the Levite and passes on the other side of the road. How much did this man know he should have helped for him to decide to intentionally walk *around* this man in order to get away?

Then we get a Levite, someone who should care for someone of his own nation, but he too walks *around* this man to get away. The priest and fellow Levite had their attention caught, but they did not decide to be intentional, and the naked and half-dead Levite cannot catch a break.

What seemed to be missing from this priest and fellow Levite was action or function. Action puts us in a state of being active and often pushes us to understand what our function is.

To this day, I enjoy building forts. There are moments when I relive some of the kid in me and pull off the cushions on my couch, the pillows and blankets on my bed, and maybe even a mattress or two, and build a fort. When the pillows, mattresses, and blankets are off the beds and couches, there is action taking place to figure out how they best fit in the fort.

Just when we think that hope is lost, and this confused lawyer still wonders who his neighbor is, Jesus mentions the

Samaritan. This man should be every lady's dream guy. Check out what he does:

"But a Samaritan, as he journeyed, came to where he was, and when he saw him, he had compassion. He went to him and bound up his wounds, pouring on oil and wine. Then he set him on his own animal and brought him to an inn and took care of him" (Luke 10:33-34 NIV).

The Samaritan man's attention immediately turned into compassion. I love the fact that this man immediately realized action needed to be taken when he saw the man. His actions were to pick up this man in the state he was in and help make him well. He did not consider his schedule or what he had to do— remember he also was traveling. He shuffled through his bag of stuff and worked to make this man as well and comfortable as he could be in that moment.

In order for us to have an intention with action, we often have to realize our function as well. With my fort-making expertise, I have found that each piece has its own specific function. The mattresses are often my base and structure because they are the strongest of the bunch, and then I have my blankets, which usually make a great covering to keep my fort somewhat private. I have my bed pillows that serve as the entrance or maybe some good flooring, depending on where I set up camp, and the couch pillows cover up some of the gaps where light could leak in.

Like the functions of the fort, this Samaritan realized his function. His action could have been good enough, especially considering that priests and brothers chose to do nothing, and Samaritans were not expected to help Levites and vice versa. This Samaritan man, however, went above and beyond.

"And the next day he took out two denarii and gave them to the innkeeper, saying, 'Take care of him, and whatever more you spend, I will repay you when I come back.' Which of these three, do you think, proved to be a neighbor to the man who fell among the robbers?" He said, "The one who showed him mercy." And Jesus said to him, "You go, and do likewise" (Luke 10:35-36 NIV).

Sometimes it can be easy for us to give our time and talents, but our treasure can be a different story. Function takes us from a place of understanding, where we know could do something to help someone to be content, to a place of helping someone feel complete. This Samaritan pulled out his own money and even promised to come back if more money was needed. Isn't that what generosity is? He said this amount could cover it but he wouldn't be content until it was paid in full. The Samaritan's function was to serve selflessly, knowing that the person he served was not of his own nation and that there likely would be no reward. His intention was to go 100 percent of the way in making sure this man was cared, rather than just a quick moment.

Notice we are not told the Samaritan's name. That is because you and I are called to be the Samaritan. God asks us how intentional we are willing to be. Are you the priest, the Levite, or the Samaritan? Remember that the priest and the Levite left this man behind, and they were people who were expected to help. Yet God used the man who should have been the passer-by, and he now is known as the Good Samaritan. Our intent to be generous should be for everyone—the people we love, the people we like, and the people we don't always like. Generous intent shouldn't be based on status or rank but on mercy. That is what will lead us to move. I am sure the left-for-dead Levite could not help but be intentional with helping out the next person he saw because of his encounter with the Good Samaritan. The generosity of the Samaritan spilled over into the life of the Levite. We all have had an encounter with the Samaritan. Even though pastors can let you down at certain points and pass you by, and people you are connected with can let you down at certain points and pass you by, God will never let you down. Even when it feels like all hope is lost, God, in His generosity, can pick you up and bring you back to life.

Having that encounter should leave us desiring and wanting to function with the same intention and action that we received. Generosity comes from God, and He is intentional, action-minded, and fully functional.

## Questions to Encourage

- What are the blessings of being intentional with generosity?
- How does God help you move your generosity from intention to action?

## The Generosity Challenge

- Pack two bag lunches, one for you and one for someone else Make a commitment to give one of the bag lunches to someone in need before you eat your own.
- Prepare a meal kit (entrée, sides, beverage) for someone you know who may be in need.

Generosity is *sacrificial.*

sac·ri·fice (ˈsakrəˌfīs), *noun*

an act of giving up something valued for the sake of
something else regarded as more important or worthy.

# 10

## Newborns and Baby Announcements

I have a feeling that if you read the chapter and section titles in the table of contents of what exactly the chapters in this book were about or maybe you just had enough confidence in the title of the book, you might have read the title of this section ("Aware, Intentional, Sacrificial, Available") and thought, *"Aware" ... yeah that sounds good. "Intentional" ... okay, no problems with that. "Sacrificial"? Great ...*

There is just something about the word sacrifice that kind of leaves us thinking we are not quite sure we are ready.

When I think of sacrifice, I cannot help but think of the parents of a newborn. I do not have a child, but from the conversations I've had with new parents, the trend seems to be very geared toward sacrifice. People say that no matter how much you try to prepare, you can't fully ready yourself for parenthood. To be honest with you, I don't think you would want to be. One of the things parents feel they most often sacrifice with a newborn in the house is a good night's sleep. I would not want to prepare for that!

They usually walk into a Sunday morning service with their faces looking a little droopy and zombie-like, and you can tell they were probably up in the early hours of the morning with their little bundle of joy. Between diaper changes, feedings, and burping, frequent checkups, fewer date nights, and the cost that goes along with these things, parenthood is incredibly sacrificial.

At the church where I work, I like to stay close to the children's department, just because those kids will someday be middle school and high school students, so why not start building that relationship now? I also like to hang around the newborns and infants because I plan on being a sacrificial parent someday. One of the most common things I see on a Sunday morning the newborn and infant area is a parent asking tons of questions of the nursery workers, as well as giving incredible amounts of information regarding their baby. These parents have every right to ask any questions they like and give any information they want. They want to know into whose hands they are leaving their babies, but we don't let just anyone run that area (and it's only for an hour-long service. You would think that the moment we take their babies into the nursery area that we take their oxygen away. It surprises me, after all the sacrifices mentioned, that parents wouldn't rejoice to have an hour alone in church with their spouses.

If you asked any parents, I'm sure they would tell you that their sacrifices are completely worth it. Sure, they have to get up earlier than usual and deal with some stinky stuff, but the love of a child is the closest thing to their hearts. I believe sacrifices can show us how close something can be to our hearts. A true sign of what we value is how much we are willing to sacrifice for it. Once you have begun to sacrifice for that, it is hard to stop. I feel like this is God's attitude toward us. He has been with us since the very beginning, since before our entrance on this earth, and He sacrificed so much so that He chooses to know the intricate and (to us) useless details, like the number of hairs on our heads. We know it is all because of His care for us. He thinks so much of us that He willingly sacrificed the closest person in His life, His son, for our sakes. It's amazing what can happen when a relationship is a priority in our lives. One of the greatest examples of sacrificial generosity was in Genesis 22 that foreshadowed what was to come when God sacrificed His Son.

To give more weight to how much of a sacrifice this really was, let me give you a little history about what was going on in the life of the person we are about to talk about. Abram (you may know him as Abraham). He was is a man who has had seen a lot of things and has had sacrificed a lot of things. I really encourage you to check out the life of Abrahamhis life in Genesis. (We can't, but in order to keep this chapter to the point we can't talk about it allhis entire life in this chapter.).

In the midst of all this, though, God gave Abram a pretty big promise.

"And I will make of you a great nation, and I will bless you and make your name great, so that you will be a blessing. I will bless those who bless you, and him who dishonors you I will curse, and in you all the families of the earth shall be blessed" (Genesis 12:2-3 NIV).

Talk about provision! God recognized Abram's sacrifice and told him to continue being obedient to God because of this promise that was to come. When Abram heard this, he was seventy-five years old and not getting any younger. Then there was Sarai, Abram's wife, who, like a good spouse, followed Abram on much of this journey but had yet to give Abram a child. She too was not getting any younger. Then, when Abram was ninety-nine years old and probably using some kind of age-defying cream, the Lord appeared to him and told him he would be the father of many nations. At this point, Abram fell on his face, and God changed his name to Abraham, which means "father of many." Here's where it gets tricky.

"And God said to Abraham, 'As for Sarai your wife, you shall not call her name Sarai, but Sarah shall be her name. I will bless her, and moreover, I will give you a son by her. I will bless her, and she shall become nations; kings of peoples shall come from her'" (Genesis 17:15-16 NIV).

Abraham does exactly what any person his age in that situation would do: he laughs. Sarah (formerly Sarai) is ninety years old. No way can she have a child. Have you ever been in a place where you sacrifice but you keep being challenged to sacrifice a little more, to believe just a little more, until it feels nearly impossible? This was that moment, where Abraham went from obedient and humbled by God to feeling humored by Him. Abraham and Sarah were that cute old couple you know who goes to your church—that couple who probably has photos of their grandkids hanging in their condo, not the type that has a baby on the way. What is so interesting about this account is how Abraham learned of Sarah's pregnancy. How many men have you known who found out about a pregnancy before their wives? That just does not happen! God was preparing Abraham for His promise—to be the father of many nations. It is amazing what can happen when someone decides to be obedient. However, Sarah had yet to hear this news. How it happened was very sitcom-like.

"The LORD said, 'I will surely return to you about this time next year, and Sarah your wife shall have a son.' And Sarah was listening at the tent door behind him. Now Abraham and Sarah were old, advanced in years. The way of women had ceased to be with Sarah. So Sarah laughed to herself, saying, 'After I am worn out, and my lord is old, shall I have pleasure?'" (Genesis 18:10-12 NIV).

You now know why these two were meant for each other—they both had the same reaction, except Sarah took a little dig at her husband. Has your sacrifice and obedience ever left you in Abraham-and-Sarah-like shock and awe? Was it to the point where it could only be God who gave you an opportunity like this to be generous or that He was the only one who could possibly make the outcome what it is? One of my youth pastors always used to say, "If your faith is not costing you anything, then it may not be worth very much." I'm not saying women should look to be pregnant at ninety years old, but I would encourage you that if you are not seeing the kinds of opportunities that put you in awe, then pray and ask God to show you those moments and give you a willingness to say yes when they come.

As for Abraham and Sarah's incredible journey, God kept His end of the promise, and when Abraham was one hundred years old, they had a son named Isaac. The name Isaac in scripture translates to "he laughs," just to remind Abraham and Sarah of how crazy this was. Just when they thought it was crazy ... it got crazier.

"After these things, God tested Abraham and said to him, 'Abraham!' And he said, 'Here I am.' He said, 'Take your son, your only son Isaac, whom you love, and go to the land of Moriah, and offer him there as a burnt offering on one of the mountains of which I shall tell you'" (Genesis 22:2 NIV).

Wouldn't it have been crazy to be a fly on the wall for this conversation? Abraham heard from God, He blessed him in his sacrifice, he has that child—and now he is asked to sacrifice that too. What in the world? Many of us don't have faith, trust, and obedience like Abraham, but we want it. We will sacrifice as much as we have to make God a priority in our lives. So Abraham woke up the next morning without any hesitation or contemplation, and he saddled up to take Isaac to the mountain. Abraham represents us, and Isaac represents our generosity. We never know exactly where God is going to lead our generosity, but it will require obedience and, most often, sacrifice. God will always make us walk sacrificially, but He will never have us give and then leave us as long as He is our reason and focus of our attention.

> When they came to the place God had told him to go to, Abraham built an altar there and laid the wood and bound Isaac his son and laid him on the altar, on top of the wood. Then Abraham reached out his hand and took the knife to slaughter his son. But the angel of the LORD called to him from heaven and said, "Abraham, Abraham!" And he said, "Here I am." He said, "Do not lay your hand on the boy or do anything to him, for now I know that you fear God, seeing you have not withheld your son, your only son, from me." And Abraham lifted up his eyes and looked, and behold, behind him was a ram, caught in a thicket by his horns. And Abraham went and took the ram and offered it up as a burnt offering instead of his son. So Abraham called the name of that place, "The LORD will provide"; as it is said to this day, "On the mount of the LORD it shall be provided." (Genesis 22:9-14 NIV)

The gift to Abraham for being willing to sacrifice Isaac was Isaac. Isaac was a blessing and a promise from God to Abraham because of his obedience. Did God revoke His promise? No. He showed more worth to the promise. We will never be able to comprehend the amount of blessing God is willing to give when we sacrifice. God brings all of Him to the table and brings something that we would never be able to comprehend. God is most understanding of what it means to sacrifice, and He would never have us do something that He Himself has not already done. That is what makes Him so great. So if He knows what sacrifice looks like, does that mean that when we sacrifice for His cause, He is prepared to be generous toward us someday? Whenever and wherever God calls someone, He equips. We do not need to speculate because He confirmed us from the very beginning.

Sometimes we feel like once we enter into a relationship with Jesus and the church world, we immediately give up our rights. Some of that is true, but remember all the rights that God exchanges with you. Even though this chapter discusses generosity as being sacrificial, I think God wants to know if you are willing to be obedient enough to Him to sacrifice. Sacrifice becomes so much easier when we choose to spend time hearing the voice of God and being obedient to it.

Every time Abraham was prepared to sacrifice something, God always loudly encouraged Abraham to keep pressing toward the promise. Whatever I sacrifice in order to be generous is worth whatever God has sacrificed to be generous to me. Our days are numbered on this earth, and—no offense to Abraham— my hope is that I sacrifice to be generous and make a difference today.

## Questions to Encourage

- How does God's sacrifice help you with how you sacrifice?
- How is sacrifice linked to obedience?

## The Generosity Challenge

- Volunteer for a night to help in the concessions stand during a local high school sporting event.
- For a week, make a commitment to park in the back lot of each place you stop so others can have the front parking spaces.

Generosity is *available.*

a·vail·a·ble (ə'vāləb(ə)l/), *adjective*

(of a person) not otherwise occupied; free to do something.

# 11

## Meatloaf and Men on a Cross

Cooking is not exactly my strong suit. I'm not like a terrible cook to the point that I burn Minute Rice or overcook water in a pot, but putting together entire dinners is not something I do often. There is one dish, though, that I am glad I do not know how to cook—meatloaf. I might be getting on a weird tangent here, and I will try to limit how much I passionately try to show you that meatloaf is a strange and pointless recipe. Meatloaf fans, you might want to skip this section.

First of all, I do not understand the ingredients or the shape. I feel like the day meatloaf was made, someone was in a house with an empty fridge, aside from an onion, a bottle of ketchup, some bacon, and hamburger meat. All four ingredients have a completely different texture, and an abundance of confusion happened in my mouth with the first bite I took.

Then, after those four random ingredients were put in, no other cooking utensils could be found besides a bread pan, so hey! Let's throw that all in there and put it in the oven. I know you might be telling me that all those thingsketchup, bacon, and onion are usually put on a hamburger anyways, but it just is not the same. (Plus, I'm not a fan of raw onions or ketchup on my burger.) The day meatloaf was first created was the day someone made do with what was available. The verse in 1 Corinthians that talks about all things being possible but not all things are profitable.

Our lives today seemed to be dictated by availability. "If the bank account allows it," or "If my schedule permits," or "If I can learn that in time"—these are phrases we typically use to either open or close our availability. So what hinders available generosity? What opens available generosity? What gives permission as to what is possible and what is not? Two thieves can help here.

As Jesus was being crucified and hung on a cross, two men were crucified with Him. The Bible does not mention what they did, but the significance of what they did was enough to lead both of them to the same result. One was hanging to the left of Jesus, and one was hanging to the right of Jesus. If you read through this passage of scripture casually, you can get quite a good understanding of what is happening. What people miss, because we assume Jesus is speaking to the ones that people who are casting lots for His garments, is the prayer He prays for both the gamblers *and* the criminals.

"And Jesus said, 'Father, forgive them, for they know not what they do'" (Luke 23:34 NIV).

Jesus knew what these men had done because He is omniscient and didn't wait to forgive them until they had told Him their life stories. He knew death for Him and those criminals was coming soon, and He made available generous and undeserving forgiveness. This generosity got the attention and the heart of one of the criminals, who responded and got hold of the frustration of the other criminal.

"One of the criminals who was hung railed at him, saying, "Are you not the Christ? Save yourself and us!" But the other rebuked him, saying, "Do you not fear God, since you are under the same sentence of condemnation? And we indeed justly, for we are receiving the due reward of our deeds; but this man has done nothing wrong." And he said, "Jesus, remember me when you come into your kingdom." (Luke 23:39-42 NIV)

If I knew the Savior of the world was next to me, I might have asked the same question of Him about why He hadn't decided to come off that cross and save me. This criminal did not notice, though, that Jesus actually was allowing him to have the availability to be saved; he could not seem to wrap his head around what was being made available to him, so the condition of his heart stayed hard. He focused on what could temporarily be possible instead of what eternally would be possible.

Then we have the other criminal, who responded to Jesus by understanding that he was deserving of the punishment he was receiving and understood that what Jesus was doing should not happen for any reason except that grace and mercy was made available to him. This criminal had a defining moment and made his heart available, and Jesus made His grace available.

"And he said to him, 'Truly, I say to you, today you will be with me in Paradise'" (Luke 23:43 NIV)

We never know what led this criminal to a cross, but we do know the end of his story. There are two reasons why the death of this criminal is so amazing. Jesus's generosity was available to anyone. The criminal, whose entire life was spent against the will of God, received a payout richer than anything he'd ever taken in a moment of availability. What made this possible was simply opening his heart and understanding that Jesus was the King.

Generosity is both available for you to receive and for you to give. Available hearts make for available generosity. If your heart is available, you generously open yourself up to much. I remember being in the car with my grandma when she would sing, "I've got the joy, joy, joy, joy down in my heart," and I would scream, *"Where?"* We sometimes miss that there is so much available to give and so much that can be available to be given to us. The following is what we open ourselves to when we make ourselves available to God and His Spirit:

"But the fruit of the Spirit is love, joy, peace, patience, kindness, goodness, faithfulness, gentleness, self-control; against such things there is no law. And those who belong to Christ Jesus have crucified the flesh with its passions and desires" (Galatians 5:22–24 NIV),

Available generosity is understanding that even though I will make mistakes in this life—I will sin, and human nature could get the best of me at certain points—the undeserving grace that God gives me is what makes me able to do *big* things in His name. We never have to make do with what is available because what is available is abundantly more than we could ever think, ask for, or imagine.

## Questions to Encourage

- How does a heart make itself available for generosity?
- How has someone's availability in generosity changed the course of history?

## The Generosity Challenge

- Take care of a senior citizen's lawn.
- Offer to tutor someone who may need help in a particular subject.

Generosity is *overflow.*

o·ver·flow (/ˈōvərˌflō/), *noun*

the excess or surplus not able to be
accommodated by an available space.

# 12

## Love and Waiting in Lines

When I was younger, my family didn't take too many out-of-state vacations. We would go out and do fun things together, like attending Summerfest (an annual music festival) or the Wisconsin state fair in Milwaukee or maybe traveling to Six Flags to ride terrifying roller coasters, but we usually stayed pretty close to home base. One spring, however, our family decided to head to sunny Orlando, Florida, and spend ten days in Disney World. I was pumped to visit the mouse everyone talks about so much.

Taking a trip out of state means everything is overflow from the moment you consider the vacation until the moment you get home from that vacation. First, someone books flights, hotels, rental cars, and park passes, which might be an overflow of cost, and if they aren't, chances are there is an overflow of your bank account spilling onto these reservations. Then your emotions begin to overflow with excitement, counting down the days to the trip. The night before the trip, you are stuffing your suitcase, jamming things in it while trying to stay under the airline's weight limit to avoid an extra fee. And that does not even get us to where we are going yet.

Every vacation, especially someone's first vacation, is full of overflow. You usually pack everything but the kitchen sink. I remember three things from the vacation to Florida like I was on it yesterday:

The first day we arrived at Disney World and saw the crowds, I did not know that many people existed on this earth. I bumped elbows with so many people and had so many strollers roll over my foot that day that I probably could have gone to see a doctor.

The second thing I remember wasI seemed to eat food every fifteen minutes. My stomach was definitely happy on that trip.

The last thing I remember the meet-and-greet with the Disney characters. My sister, who was pretty young when we vacationed, was enamored of these characters, as if they were the real things, and other people's kids felt the same way. We stood in line in the hot sun in the same spot for hours, praying that either the line or the character would disappear. The crazier part is that as I sit in Wisconsin today, I would still vacation to Florida, character visits included. That trip was so much fun and even had a hint of being life-changing for me.

I was exposed to what fullness really looked like by being in one of the busiest places in the entire world. Unlike being at a DMV, almost every person there was happy to be in a place of overflow. Yet that does not even compare to the kind of overflow that God is used to having. How big does heaven need to be to house all the believers who are going to be with Him? Or the fact that the earth is the size that it is to fit God's creation in it. I love how personal God gets, even after mentioning just a small portion of what He does.

> For this reason I bow my knees before the Father,
> from whom every family in heaven and on earth
> is named, that according to the riches of his glory

he may grant you to be strengthened with power through his Spirit in your inner being, so that Christ may dwell in your hearts through faith—that you, being rooted and grounded in love, may have strength to comprehend with all the saints what is the breadth and length and height and depth, and to know the love of Christ that surpasses knowledge, that you may be filled with all the fullness of God. Now to him who is able to do far more abundantly than all that we ask or think, according to the power at work within us, to him be glory in the church and in Christ Jesus throughout all generations, forever and ever. Amen. (Ephesians 3:14-21 NIV)

The above scripture passage mentions the word "you" and how God desires to make a connection with you five times. God wants to cram, jam, and fill every part of your life with generosity. From the moment your life was planned, He was already stuffing your life with an overflow of every good thing He has. He wants to cater to you and expand you to the point where you cannot contain yourself, and generosity just spills out from your life onto others. There's a point in this prayer where Paul actually prays that we are ready for this amount of overflow because it is so intense it could sweep you off your feet. He is at work, doing this for each individual person all at once. You do not need to pack your bags and move to receive it; you do not need to stand in line to wait for it. All you need to do is understand the power of the work that is going on within you. Will you allow Paul's prayer to be your prayer for your life? Will you allow this to be your prayer for other people's lives? Once this happens, your overflow starts with the center space for your generosity—your heart. Love is what pushes us to generosity, and love is the essence of who God is.

## Questions to Encourage

- How do you feel overflow as you learn how to give?
- How is generous overflow linked to joy?

## The Generosity Challenge

- Gather old clothes that you do not wear anymore, and donate them to an organization that specializes in taking care of the homeless.
- Spend the day offering your assistance in a special-needs classroom.

# Given + Forgiven
# Robber + Steward
# Future Promises

# 13

## Why Am I Doing This?

I was a pretty decent student in high school. I wasn't the valedictorian or even the salutatorian, but I could hold my own. English was my strong suit, and I was decent at history and science. We all had that one class, though, that seemed to tank our grade point average, gave us countless nights of frustration, and led us to burning that particular text as soon as we had freedom from its captivity—you may know what I mean. For me, this was the not-so-wonderful world of math. I loathed even the thought of walking into my math class, and it felt like air was sucked out of the room every time I sat at my desk.

My math skills were so bad that during my junior year in high school, I had to pray that my math teacher would have mercy on me and pass me in her class. I went to a Christian school, and thank God for that, because she did pass me—but she didn't let me off the hook without first suggesting that I should consider taking basic math my senior year. Ouch. I still do not quite understand why I am so bad at math. My dad is an accountant, so he works with numbers all the time. Also, there was a time when I was good at math and enjoyed it. Now, I try to stay away from it as much as possible and even went into ministry to avoid numbers (okay, that definitely was not the deciding factor, but it helped seal that calling on my life). I remember sitting in my math class, knowing what my plan was for ministry, and thinking to myself, *Why am I doing this? Why am I opening myself up to be frustrated?* I'd walk out of class, day after day, feeling like I just got a concussion. *Who cares about numbers anyway?* I thought. *I won't ever use the Pythagorean theorem in my job.*

I think sometimes this is how we feel about being people of generosity. We enjoyed being generous when it made sense to us. For some of us, though, at some point in time the process became a little fuzzy, and so we let generosity take a backseat, to the point where now we don't even get what the point of it is. We ask ourselves questions like, "Why should I bother being generous? Nobody acknowledges me when I try to be nice to them. I am just one person in a big giant world. My generosity is not going to change anything." If we look at generosity as a problem of people not showing enough of it, we will never choose to be the solution. We cannot force people to be generous, just like my math teacher could not force me to take an additional math class the next year because I had enough math credits. So much discussion is always put around changing the world. I can appreciate the courage and motivation, and I love to dream big; it is even a phrase I have said in this book multiple times already, but it can be overwhelming! And because it's overwhelming, it probably makes a lot of people want to quit before they even ever start.

How many times do you hear about changing just one person? As weird as this might sound, I don't think God has levels of excitement. I think He is just plain excited! He loves each individual person with an unending kind of love, so whenever anyone comes to Him, He is thrilled. How many more people would be motivated if they knew they were called to be generous to even just one person? I still am not good at math, but I know that if each one of us would reach just one, the kingdom of God would double!

You might be called to great things. You might be called to be an accountant or a lawyer or a police officer, and those are great professions, but first you are called to people. And God could be bringing someone your way, someone who is called to hear God's life-changing gospel from you.

When it comes to giving, you might not be good at math, but God has given you different skills and talents. You might fail in areas of life, but you should not beat yourself up because God has forgiven you. You shouldn't quit on your plans and people because God has future promises for you. That's why I want to be a person of generosity. I didn't take that additional math class, and I sometimes wonder if choosing to take it would have given me the key to unlocking whatever it was about math that left me confused. But there is one math problem I love because I know the answer: God + One = the Majority.

I have been *given* and *forgiven* more than I could ever *give.*

# 14

## Car Dealers and Indescribable Worth

### *Given and Forgiven*

When we do not understand our worth, we miss out on the fullness of what God desires to give us. We often put a cap on how much of the fullness of God we allow ourselves to take in. It is a hard street to walk down, considering that there are more things on this earth that try to lower our value than raise it. However, when we do position ourselves to receive more than we normally allow ourselves to be given, we are exponentially more joyful and prepared to invest and show others what we have been given.

Recently, I went to look at some cars. My car really is two years old, but I realized that a 2013 Dodge Avenger is not exactly an ideal Wisconsin car, and this winter I want to be more safe than sporty. I went into the dealership just to see what my possible trade-in value would be for my car. I have loved having my Avenger—heated leather seats, custom sound system, touch-screen dash. I am not trying to brag here; I have just been blessed. However, to the dealership this was not the major factor in estimating my car's worth. The worth of the car was based on one thing: miles. And there are many miles on my car because of two things: (1) a ninety-minute round trip to work each day; and (2) ministry traveling.

Therein lies the harsh reality I got at the dealership that day for my two-year-old Avenger. The value I put on the car was way more than the value they put on it. Leaving the dealership, I understood why I put such a high value on my car. It was the first car I ever made payments on, and it was the first car I drove off the lot that now had a cost to me because of its value.

When we evaluate our own lives, we often put ourselves in the place of the car dealers. We are harsh critics of our own lives and ask questions like the following:

- How often do I consider other people?
- Am I doing and saying the right things?
- Is my life consistent across the board?
- How am I using my time?
- Do God, my family, and the people closest to me approve of what I do?
- Do I always give in to temptations?
- If people were to open a book that was my life, would they be inspired?

And slowly we become our greatest critics, and we lessen the value of our lives. We think there is no way that we can possibly take the sum of the answers to the above questions and trade them in for what was already a free gift of forgiveness. Our view of our worth can get in the way of the influence we have.

Malachi is a great example of someone who understands how the view of someone's worth can get in the way. In the Bible, Malachi is a messenger; it is actually what his biblical name means. He is working with a group of Israelites who have it all going for them. From anyone else's point of view, it probably looked like an ideal situation. Money, chariots, jewelry—you name it; they probably have it. They might be externally loaded, but it appears they are missing the mark, and Malachi gives them this message:

"'I the LORD do not change. So you, the descendants of Jacob, are not destroyed. Ever since the time of your ancestors you have turned away from my decrees and have not kept them. Return to me, and I will return to you,' says the LORD Almighty" (Malachi 3:6-7 NIV).

Clearly, the Israelites were in a place where they seemed to have it all, but there was a clear void in their lives. Even though there was prosperity for them, none of that could take the place of what they once received from God.

We often look at money, possessions, job advancements, and the array of other things in this life that can move us forward as the true example of the generous hand of God at work. Before you disagree and close this book, God does bless us but are you completely convinced that God's priority is worrying about how we can find our value on this Earth? I'm not so sure. I think God is preparing us to understand our value to Him before we meet Him someday. What He wants to return to us is substantially more than what we can return to Him. He is not a God that negotiates with us or bases what He plans to give us on the demands we meet. He is not a commission-based God. We are free receivers when we return to Him.

Since the beginning of time, no one has ever been able to live up to the standards that God truly wants us to have in our lives. I'm not saying we shouldn't strive for that standard; if you think about it, it is more for our benefit than for His. The standard is so much easier when you understand what has been done because God saw how valuable you truly are. I am so glad God doesn't base how much He chooses to give us on the trade-in value of our lives. If He were to ever measure our lives based on a scale of dos and don'ts, we would never have access to all that He wants to offer us. We have a hard time living and giving generously because we have a problem believing that God is real in our lives.

When we give to God our brokenness and high-mileage sin, it may be hard to believe that He would place an insurmountable value on that. But just like the high value I put on my car, God puts a high value on our lives because He created us. He sees our worth differently than the world or anyone else sees it. The one thing that we can offer Him—our relationship to Him—is worth all the love, care, and compassion that He would give to us. When we understand how to freely receive God's gifts, we will understand how to be generous with our earthly gifts.

Freely you have received; now freely will you give?

## Questions to Motivate

- How does grace help in your journey for living a generous life?
- What is one great moment of generosity that you were able to be a part of?

## The Generosity Challenge

- Write a note thanking a veteran for his or her service to our country.
- Spend time greeting and welcoming people at a place where people do not expect to be greeted (DMV, post office, grocery store).

# 15

## Stolen Goods and Stewardship

### *Robber and Steward*

Have you ever been robbed? Most people likely haven't been a victim, so for the sake of helping everyone to relate, let's bring stealing to its simplest form. Has anyone ever taken the Ben & Jerry's ice cream that had your name written in Sharpie marker all over it? Maybe someone stole your time—that's something you will never get back. Put that way, chances are that something has been stolen from most of us—and we possibly have stolen from other people.

One moment I will never forget is when I some things were stolen from me. I was finishing up the first semester of my freshman year of college. One night I was hanging out with some friends just a few doors down from my room. My roommate came into the room I was hanging out in and asked me if I if I'd seen his computer anywhere. He had a huge laptop, so I didn't understand how it could have gone missing. I decided to check the room myself, and that's when I realized my things were missing too. After shuffling through my room I realized what was stolen, —my laptop, backpack, glasses, and savings bonds. My night quickly became both blurry and frustrating.

Nobody likes it when their things are taken. Being robbed is a quick way to unlock someone's inner Sherlock Holmes and demand that justice to be served. We work hard for what we have and often spend extra hours working or save up for a long time to buy what we want. Anyone who has an ounce of morality would say, "Why in the world would anyone deliberately take something from someone?" I can only imagine how God feels, considering that we do this to Him on a daily basis. We live our lives, forgetting who our source is and believe that we can be better managers of what we have than He is, the one who provided us with what we manage. It is daring that we decide to do that!

Remember Malachi? He warned the hard-headed Israelites about their missing the point when it came to understanding who should be their priority. They were so consumed with what they had and what they had been doing that they didn't know how to return to God, but they wanted to know what was up, so they asked,

"How are we to return?'

"Will a mere mortal rob God? Yet you rob me.

"But you ask, 'How are we robbing you?' (Malachi 3:8 NIV)

It is not humanly possible for someone to be selfish and generous at the same time. Have you ever known someone who offers a million answers to a question that is straightforward and simple? The Israelites were completely clueless because they had spent so much time being selfish. They had robbed God for so long that they didn't understand what they were doing anymore.

Now try to forgive someone who does this on a consistent basis. It's hard to wrap our minds around the fact that God chooses to give forgiveness to us, regardless of the number of times we choose to rob from Him.

So how do we get to this place where we steal from our Savior? Selfishness is probably one of the first thoughts that pops into our minds. I simply do not want to give to anyone else because it is mine, and who knows if I can trust that person with what I give him? Have you ever been part of a project that involved a group of people? You set up a game plan for how the project will go, and you assign people their tasks. But what happens when one part of the project doesn't get done? One specific person catches the heat from the group because he or she quit. Chances are, that person will not be trusted to do anything else, and the rest of the group will second-guess giving that person any more responsibility. God has every reason to not trust us. Just like the Israelites, we rob from God when we quit on the project Jesus gives us to lead this world to Him.

One of the most frequent conversations I have with students begins with the question, "Why would God?" I think that can be a valid question. Our world feels constantly cluttered with family circumstances, job situations, or simply feeling overwhelmed with all the noise in our lives. I find that when I ask that question for my own life, I open the door for myself to reason with God. Reasoning can cloud our ability to trust. I want legitimate answers, and I don't always receive them. And when relationships are based on trust, my relationship with God can feel clouded too.

It is easy for Satan to use this world as his platform to make us feel disappointed with God. A symptom of our not being convinced of God is that we think we can produce good on our own. Moral living can be great, but at some point we come at a crossroads, wondering what it's worth. When we find ourselves passionately in love with God and the position He holds in our lives, we become convinced of Him. And when we are convinced of Him, we are willing to do anything for Him.

We actually begin to think of more ways we can be generous to God and to people. Do you find yourself eager to give? I definitely want to feel more led to be a steward of God's than a robber. God has already invested enough of Himself in the project of our lives for us to be convinced of Him. Remember my story about my stuff being stolen from me? It wasn't anyone from the school, which I discovered when I watched the footage of a surveillance tape. And I kicked myself because I had walked right past the people who stole from me! My situation had a good ending, though, because my dad had homeowner's insurance. I ended up receiving compensation that was more than what my items were worth and was blessed to be able to upgrade what was stolen. I never got a chance to thank the people who stole my stuff, but maybe someday I will. I want God to be my homeowner. When I place my life in His hands, He does more with it than I could ever do on my own. Hang with me on this next phrase—for that reason I want to be a *Stuart* and not a *Robert.*

## Questions to Motivate

- Other than finances, where are other areas where stewardship exists?
- At what point does generous stewardship become more than moral?

## The Generosity Challenge

- Take a coworker out to lunch.
- Pick up the grocery bill for the person in front of you in line.

# 16

## Jobs and Jesus's Promises

### *I Want to Be a Part of His Future Promises*

When I strive and live to give and to be a steward for God's plan, I also see God's future promises. When I started my senior year in college, I had an idea of where I wanted to live when I became a youth pastor. I'd been to Colorado, and it had taken my breath away, so I thought it would be awesome to head west and do youth ministry there. I started looking at churches in Colorado that wanted someone brand new to ministry, someone willing to give forgiveness for any mistakes made. I wasn't really concerned with where God wanted me to be as much as where I thought it would be ideal. Halfway into my senior year, a friend with whom I was doing ministry got an alert about a position that was open in Wisconsin. When he told me about it, I blew him off immediately because I had my future set. What I thought would be my future, however, was not what God had for my future promise. After much personal debate, I finally made the phone call to what is now the church where I do youth ministry, the church I call home.

It is much easier to be obedient when you know the end result of the decision for which you are being obedient. We are creatures of completion, meaning we like to think with the end in mind. But when a decision requires faith, we wish we could know the process. God understands what we are going through because throughout scripture He always presented the promise. The process, however, is usually where we find ourselves feeling stuck. Stephen could probably understand how painful the process can be.

In Jesus's time, there were many disciples, but the day-to-day work of taking care of widows and orphans was often neglected. Enter Stephen, who became one of seven dudes who helped with the day-to-day duties. Stephen was close to the Lord and did signs and wonders, which left teachers of the law disputing with Stephen. This guy, who was just living out the way he was called by God with obedience, was left with a false-witness charge. Stephen took an obedient stand, but through others' false testimony and jealousy, he received the greatest punishment.

Stephen's faithful obedience led him to the future promise of death. This doesn't sound like a very convincing point for me to live generously. No, it does not sound all that great, but before you get set in that thought, read on.

But he, full of the Holy Spirit, gazed into heaven and saw the glory of God, and Jesus standing at the right hand of God. And he said, "Look, I see the heavens opened, and the Son of Man standing at the right hand of God" (Acts 7:55-56 NIV).

Amazing, right? We think it is torture, but Stephen sees a future promise waiting for him. And the best part is that Jesus is there with Stephen as he goes through the process, almost as if He's showing Stephen that what he is going through will be worth it. It takes a lot to find something satisfying enough that we would find it worth dying for, and Jesus showed that to Stephen. Stephen's name in scripture means "crown." The promise that Jesus was preparing for Stephen was made even before this moment when Stephen went to meet Him.

What the promise led Stephen to do is mind-boggling—like trying to understand calculus when you are not good at math. Stephen, as he was being stoned to death, made the following statement:

"And as they were stoning Stephen, he called out, 'Lord Jesus, receive my spirit.' And falling to his knees he cried out with a loud voice, 'Lord, do not hold this sin against them.' And when he had said this, he fell asleep" (Acts 7:59-60 ESV).

Sounds like someone else we know and love. When you understand the value of the promise, that's all that matters. Jesus did this same thing for us. Salvation was the promise, and the cost was worth it because the relationship has value. He gives us something to strive for and then partners with us on the process. It is a win/win situation because we get to see reward and have deeper relationship with Him. I could not imagine my life today without the church in which I have the opportunity to do ministry. God's plans were greater than my plans and still are greater than my plans. Being able to invest in the people of Poplar Creek Church and having a small part in the changing and shaping of their lives is better than any mountain range in Colorado on which I could pull back the curtains. The promise even allows us to generous to our enemies.

Does the future promise push you to generosity? Does your Savior leave you wanting to make a statement of love, even to your enemies? We are constantly presented with opportunities in this life to be generous, and our deeper relationship with Jesus grows when He is present in our process.

Faithful obedience can equal future opportunity.

## Questions to Motivate

- How does generosity point to the promise?
- What do you believe are God's promises for you?

## The Generosity Challenge

- Buy a five-dollar or ten-dollar gas card, and let someone know his or her drive to work or church is on you that day
- Give a care package to a college student and encourage his or her pursuit of education.

# Time
# Resources
# Riches

# 17

## It's Not the What; It's the How

Have you ever received something that held a lot of sentimental value to you? It might not have been something that cleaned out someone's bank account, but it holds a high value to you. My grandma was all about gifts that had sentimental value. The cost of a gift was the last thing on her mind. When her birthday or Christmas rolled around each year, we would give her expensive gifts, but we always knew the one gift that would leave her in tears would be a framed picture of her kids and grandkids. We would joke that it was time to get out the mop so that we could soak up all her tears. Every time my grandma opened up that gift, she was moved to tears because that that picture contained every loving feeling that we felt toward her. It showed my grandma that we appreciated her sacrifices and her generosity and wanted to show that to her.

Maybe you can relate to moments you have spent with your own family, honoring that person or people who may be the glue for the family, keeping them coming together and being connected. For us, that person was Grandma.

My grandma was a woman of incredible faith. I have never seen someone battle stage-four cancer, open-heart surgeries, and other health issues with such courage and confidence that

God was taking care of her. A lot of us felt she was immortal. She made sure that no matter what circumstance we faced, we knew not to focus on *what* we were dealing with but *how* we would deal with it and the attitude we would have toward it. I remember sitting around her kitchen table talking with her. She often would say two things: "Fight the good fight of faith," and "It's not the what; it's the how."

This has become somewhat of an anthem for my life, and I tell it to my students all the time. Jesus said that in this life we will face circumstances, but "take heart I have overcome the world." Life circumstances are the what; Jesus's overcoming the world is the how. We have figured out what generosity is, but now it's time to figure out how we can be generous. We can spend all our lives working to do good things, meet our expectations, be accomplished, and be successful, and those are all good things. The "what" of generosity that we choose to give to God, though, is something He already owns because He is the ruler of all. The "what" of generosity to Him is a return given to Him as our way of saying thank you. Jesus is more attentive to the "how" we can give because that is closely connected to our hearts. Our things are not relational with God, but hopefully our hearts are. My grandma really loved us with her whole heart, but it was just an ounce of how God truly feels about us.

Whatever your standing is in life—your past, your present, or where you are going with your future—know again that you are capable of being generous. You might feel like you are better at giving in certain areas, and that is completely okay. You may not feel as strong in one or two areas, but my hope is that you are encouraged. I hope that you challenge yourself to step outside of your comfort zone and strategize and discipline yourself in ways that see you giving stronger in those areas. My prayer for you, as you read these next few chapters on how to be generous, is that you can find new, exciting, innovative, and world-changing ideas that affect the trajectory of people's lives forever. God is a sentimental God, and He loves the heart and attitude of the gifts we give to Him.

Generosity is your *time.*

# 18

## License to Build

I'm a timely person—I choose to be timely. There are a couple reasons why I choose to be a timely person. One of them is that When I was growing up, my family was never on time (sorry to my mom and dad, if you are reading this but we know this is true). I enjoyed being a part of Church church activities and started tobut gained the reputation as the one most people expected to be late for a service project, event, or trip. That all changed the day that I got my driver's license. I remember that asAs I was holding thatheld it identification in my hand, I felt it was also the seal of approval for me that I did not need to be late another day in my life. Now, between appointments, students and their events, meetings, and a personal life, I have realized that time just might be my greatest asset.

I'm not sure when the emphasis of time became such a key part of my life, but I do know that we all get twenty-four hours in a day. No one is blessed with more time in a day or has the ability to stop the clock, so God must see our influential ability and capability as equal. How we choose to spend those twenty-fours is what makes that time valuable and determines how much of a difference we allow ourselves to make. Because time is the one thing we can't get more of, generosity often begins with the commitment to give our time. Have you ever spent time on Netflix and got caught up in a TV series? I have—I know that it's likely that when I check the time, two or three hours will have passed.

There are plenty of things on this earth that want to hoard our time, and this exactly how the devil wants it. He wants to slowly pull you away from what opens up the generosity inside of you by taking the one thing you are limited with: time. We need to be careful because if the devil can pull us away from the time we have to identify our identity in Christ, he will win the battle against our influence. Our time on this earth is borrowed, and we are managers of what we have. God has given each of us a purpose to use that time. We cannot manufacture more time, but we can learn how to manage it. And we have the opportunity with our time to build or break.

Have you ever been on a boat, maybe a speedboat or a cruise ship? I love the water, but I'm not a boat expert. I would guess the average size of a boat is eighteen to twenty feet. It probably holds four to six people comfortably, with a little room to move around and hang out. Then I am reminded of a boat that held a family of eight. That must have been a pretty decent-sized boat, right? Oh, and it also held two of every animal on the earth. This sounds like it consumed a lot of space, and if it will consume space, it will consume time.

Noah was this guy who, according to scripture, was a righteous dude and walked with God. I'm sure he put the time in every day for prayer, worship, and reverence to God. I'm sure he had his to-do list and plans (hang out with the kids, mow the lawn, pick up groceries) until God showed up with a task that completely flipped Noah's concept of time.

And God said to Noah, "I have determined to make an end of all flesh, for the earth is filled with violence through them. Behold, I will destroy them with the earth. Make yourself an ark of gopher wood. Make rooms in the ark, and cover it inside and out with pitch. This is how you are to make it: the length of the ark 300 cubits, its breadth 50 cubits, and its height 30 cubits. Make a roof for the ark, and finish it to a cubit above, and set the door of the ark in its side. Make it with lower, second, and third decks. For behold, I will bring a flood of waters upon the earth to destroy all flesh in which is the breath of life under heaven. Everything that is on the earth shall die. But I will establish my covenant with you, and you shall come into the ark, you, your sons, your wife, and your sons' wives with you. And of every living thing of all flesh, you shall bring two of every sort into the ark to keep them alive with you. They shall be male and female. Of the birds according to their kinds, and of the animals according to their kinds, of every creeping thing of the ground, according to its kind, two of every sort shall come in to you to keep them alive. Also take with you every sort of food that is eaten, and store it up. It shall serve as food for you and for them." (Genesis 6:13-21 ESV)

This is the moment in scripture where I wish I could have been a fly on the wall. I can imagine Noah saying, "Well, I guess I better clear out my schedule then." Since cubits aren't the measurement system today, I'll put it in modern terms. We are talking 450 feet long, 75 feet wide, and 45 feet high. This boat was like a floating mansion! Noah got ready to commit his

89

time to a process that would be days, nights, and weekends. To anyone else, this might have been absolutely crazy, and based on everyone's mocking Noah, they did think he was crazy. But for Noah, this was understanding a purpose and a plan. God told Noah that his family would be with him and kept safe, and two of every animal would come in to be kept alive. Time attached to a purpose and a plan becomes different because it becomes more effective. I'm sure that long hours on a hot day, with the sun beating down and a few hammer hits to the thumb, could have left any of us wanting to give up, but Noah believed in the plan. Committing incredible amounts of time and seeing very little progress on a lofty ark-sized goal could have left Noah seeing if anyone in the area was offering swimming lessons, but Noah trusted the process. Do we believe in the plan? Do we trust the process? Or when it comes to doing what we feel God has asked us to do, do we feel like we are running late or falling behind?

It can be easy to give generosity a backseat because it takes intentional effort (or because we are consumed by our clocks), but a God-centered vision brings about a God-centered value.

*Noah did this; he did all that God commanded him.*

## Questions to Consider

- What is the majority of your time focused on? How can you make time for generosity?
- How does making God a priority in your life change how you spend your time?

## The Generosity Challenge

- Spend some time with someone in a nursing home. Ask the person a little bit about his or her life and just listen. You may be surprised at what you find out.
- Give your friends an opportunity for a date night by watching their kids, free of charge

Generosity is your *resource.*

# 19

## TV Shows and Sharing Resources

Reality TV singing shows seem to be all the rage these days. Whether it is season forty-five of *American Idol* or being crowned on the *X Factor*, these shows seem to capture the hearts, tweets, Facebook statuses, and text-to-votes from America. Lately, I have been intrigued by *The Voice*. Contestants belt out songs onstage, doing their best to capture the ears and heart of one of the four judges. What makes it interesting is that none of the judges can see the person who is singing. The judges may be so impressed that they press a button, their chairs turn, and they now see the person singing. If more than one chooses the same contestant, they then battle with each other, using their array of accomplishments to convince that particular person to be on their team. The audition is based completely on approval. Once the person picks a coach, he or she is voted on, week after week. If they gain America's approval, they stay, and if not, they are eliminated.

For all of us, approval is something everyone works hard for. We always try to live by doing and saying the right things at the right time. Often we use our resources to have the edge on gaining approval. It is amazing how much someone's approval of us can change over the course of a week. We are emotional beings, so when we are disappointed by someone, we disapprove, and our chairs are not turned toward that person. Even though we already have God's approval, many of us seem to use our talents to seek God's approval. I don't know why we do that. Maybe it is because we see God as an intimidating coach who will judge and remark on every little misstep that we make. But He is always moved in our direction. He understands that if none of us ever used our talents, we would miss out on an essential part of the creativity and wonder of God. He has shared those talents because He wants to see those talents!

Romans 12:3–11 sums it up in the best way possible. We all have something to offer because of what we have been offered.

> For by the grace given to me I say to everyone among you not to think of himself more highly than he ought to think, but to think with sober judgment, each according to the measure of faith that God has assigned. For as in one body we have many members, and the members do not all have the same function, so we, though many, are one body in Christ, and individually members one of another. Having gifts that differ according to the grace given to us, let us use them: if prophecy, in proportion to our faith; if service, in our serving; the one who teaches, in his teaching; the one who exhorts, in his exhortation; the one who contributes, in generosity; the one who leads, with zeal; the one who does acts of mercy, with cheerfulness. Let love be genuine. Abhor what is evil; hold fast to what is good. Love one another with brotherly affection. Outdo one another in showing honor. Do not be slothful in zeal, be fervent in spirit, serve the Lord. (Romans 12:3-11 ESV)

God has given us something we can share with others. Our resources are meant to be shared. If we had nothing to share or offer, we would have a pretty lousy purpose here on earth. God even uses an analogy to which we can all relate—the human body. That is how interested He is in the investment of our resources. And generous resources will not point to the created but to the Creator. So how do we make and give this investment back to the Creator? I think it begins with understanding that we are all part of one body, and that one body is God's. God gives each of us a pep talk for talents. Remember the Nike slogan, "Just do it"? God's slogan when it comes to our talents is "Just use it!" An unused talent is a useless talent. The next thing He asks us to do is to serve Him with it.

If you played sports as a kid, you might remember that moment in a game when your parents were cheering for you like crazy. That was my mom. I would probably have been embarrassed by most of what she said, had it not been for the fact that I was in a competitive game of basketball or flag football. She never particularly cheered for my team as much as she cheered for me, specifically. She cheered for me because I was her son. All the fans in the stands knew full well when I was in the game. God enjoys seeing us use the talent He gives us, and He becomes that wired, loud, and excited sideline parent. He runs down the field with you as you generously serve this world with the resources you have. Why? Because it was God-given. And nothing excites God more than to see you serve and live with what He has given you. He knows it is another open door to a relationship with Him and introducing the world to Him.

So use your talents, and use them frequently. If you are good at music, maybe you could teach others how to play, or join a worship team at the church you attend. Maybe you are very hospitable, and so you open up your home and allow people to feel welcomed and received like never before. We have a God who is limitless. He takes our talents and makes those resources become much more than we could ever dream or imagine.

*There is no limit to what God can do with your resources.*

## Questions to Consider

- How does knowing God's approval for generosity change the way you approach generosity?
- How could your resources and talent influence the way you are generous toward others?

## The Generosity Challenge

- Ask your local church or a nonprofit organization who may need some help, and volunteer your help to them.
- Make a dessert for a neighbor.

Generosity is your *riches.*

# 20

## Paychecks and Offering Plates

Remember getting your first paycheck? I do, and man, that was one of the greatest feelings on the planet! Sure, you did not want to work those ten long, grueling hours during the weekend, when you were folding clothes while everyone else was having a social life. It all paid off (no pun intended), though, the minute you ripped open that envelope and saw the fruit of all your labor.

You feel so good receiving what you have earned, but how eager are you to give it back to God? Tithes and offerings seem to be one of the "taboo" things that every pastor works around to keep people happy and in the church. It's the sermon that happens once a year and makes the pastor sweat through both his shirt and his deodorant. We shy away from talking about riches because it offends some people and makes them feel like there is a scale of worth, according to how much we give. I won't do that. I believe God wants to show and share with us that our riches are His riches. God wants to show us that it is not what we give but the manner in how we plan to give it. God wants to show His faithfulness to us in expressions that go well beyond what our 10 percent could ever do. This chapter is meant to help you learn how to give—and maybe you will find yourself so excited about your heart that it will extend to your pockets. If He can work through a widow, He can work through us!

Mark 12:41–44 shows us exactly how God views giving—I mean, His Son was in the story.

"Jesus sat down opposite the place where the offerings were put and watched the crowd putting their money into the temple treasury. Many rich people threw in large amounts" (Mark 12:41 NIV).

So here we have an opportunity to see what Jesus is really all about. Jesus sat on the opposite side of this temple treasury, but for modern times' sake, let's just call it the offering bucket. Many rich people came—today they would compare to our CEOs and business leaders, maybe a few celebrities, and a boy band—and put serious Benjamins in the plate. I am sure a few of the people who knew who Jesus and noticed Him probably wanted to represent, so maybe they slid in some extra money, just to show Jesus how generous they were willing to be. What these people did not understand was that He seemed unconcerned by what they put in, considering that He was sitting opposite the offering box. Then we notice something that captured not only Jesus's attention but also His heart.

"But a poor widow came and put in two very small copper coins, worth only a few cents" (Mark 12:42 NIV).

Here comes this poor old widow, who probably doesn't get the time of day from any of the rich executives who are putting in big checks. She makes her way to the offering bucket and puts in everything that she has. If you are like me, you have a tendency to think with your stomach. This offering given is considered the most generous because it means she potentially won't be eating for one or maybe even two days, but it was worth it to her because her God was worth serving in that way. This woman displayed life-changing generosity, even though she put in the least amount of money out of the bunch.

We all have something to give because generosity is our riches. If we value something, chances are we get a warranty on it, make sure it's always near us, and make sure to take care of it. Notice that it does not say the amount of the riches. It's not the numbers in your salary per year or the amount of time you invest in your local church. The amount of relationship, resources, and riches given does not dictate the God you serve, but the heart in which you give and to whom you give dictates the God you serve. Luke 12:34 says, "Where your treasure is, there your heart will be also" (NIV).

This woman defines generosity because her heart is drawn to give, even until it hurts. What makes this story even more incredible is one small detail that we tend to miss. This story is about a widow. This indicates that this woman had a husband whom she lost at some point. Losing someone can be one of the most difficult and painful times in someone's life. This woman potentially could have been in the situation she was in financially because she had lost her husband, leaving her heart bitter or angry. In short time I have been in ministry, there have been many occasions when people have turned their backs on God because of their losses. The widow lost what was quite possibly the closest person to her, and she could have given her generosity a second thought, but without hesitation she chose to give.

"Calling His disciples to him, Jesus said, 'Truly I tell you, this poor widow has put more into the treasury than all the others. They all gave out of their wealth; but she, out of her poverty, put in everything—all she had to live on'" (Mark 12:43–44 NIV).

Have you ever worked incredibly hard for that one thing that completely catches your attention? As a kid, I wanted to learn how to play the guitar. I envisioned myself as the next greatest guitar player, learning how to shred on it, being in a band, and being the most famous guy on the planet. I did not know at the time, but it was pretty clear that my sister got all the musical gifts. I just got the gift of being really tall and really bad at hide-and-seek. I remember mowing the lawn, washing and drying dishes, and even vacuuming the carpet to earn money. After many weeks of working around the house, I walked into the guitar store, locked my eyes on the ocean-blue Fender guitar, and took it home that day. I left that day with no money—I put in every cent I had—but with a brand-new guitar.

That guitar was definitely a beginner, just like my guitar skills, but to me it was the best guitar in the world. The price did not matter to me; I'd have paid twice as much for it, and I would have worked even longer to get it. What made this guitar my treasure was that it completely wiped out my eight-year-old bank account! The number of hours I put into getting that guitar is what made it great. The cost of an iPad or new Nikon camera that you are looking to get doesn't matter as much as its cost to the giver.

When it comes to your generosity toward Jesus, it is great that you are giving, and I pray that you are incredibly blessed with whatever you do give. When it comes to Jesus and generosity, however, when was the last time you gave until it hurt? When was the last time you gave when it meant holding off on going to Chick-Fil-A for the next few rounds? When did your giving put your Macbook Pro fund on hold?

The hardest one for me, when it comes to the "Where your treasure is, there your heart will be also" guideline, is my skill. Some of us might be pro athletes, musicians, gamers, artists, or something else. And when we have skills, it is easy to want to invest in those skills. We spend extra time on the practice field, in the art room, unlocking achievements on our Xboxes, or buying new games or sporting or art equipment. I am not knocking your gifts, and you should know that it is not wrong to invest in your skills because they are a gift from God. We tend to forget, though, that our skills are not God Himself. Come on— God has enough skills already! Many of us sacrifice, hoping our skills get us closer to God, when God is more concerned about having us than our skills.

Jesus immediately told His disciples, His twelve closest friends, that the widow was doing things right. I can only imagine what these rich people would have thought if they ever overheard Jesus's conversation with the disciples about this poor old widow. Jesus wants your heart. Jesus is far more concerned with your heart, faith, and treasure than with the amount you can give. All three of these things point to His desire to have a relationship with you. Often these three things with which Jesus is concerned lead us to a place where we need to decide whether we will sacrifice and if we are willing to sacrifice all of us. At this place in your life, have you found the faith to give God your future? Your finances? I can only imagine the reward that was waiting for the poor old widow when she finally met Jesus again in heaven!

*It pays to give.*

## Questions to Consider

- How does heavenly wealth help you to be generous financially?
- In what ways are your heart and treasure connected?

## The Generosity Challenge

- For one week, spend time just drinking water and use the money that would normally have been used to buy specialty drinks (coffee, energy drinks, etc.) for your church offering.
- Grab ten dollars in quarters, and hand them out to people at your local Laundromat.

# 21

## Strategize, Serve, Save

In this book, I've mostlyMost of this book has been spent talking explaining explained and sharing shared about the what's, whys, and how's of generosity. If you are anything like me, though, I you live off a plan. I seem to succeed and fail based on whether or not I have a plan. When If I fail to plan, I typically essentially plan to fail. Of course, Generosity generosity comes up in spur spur-of of-the moment situations, but if I were to create a game plan for generosity, it would wraps around these three words:. strategize, serve, and save.

### Strategize

Have you ever watched a team put together a game plan? I love sports and have grown to like watching and figuring the different plays that a football team or a basketball team draws up. There is just something about following through on a perfect plan that gets people excited and motivated, but the plan does not happen immediately. Hours and hours are spent looking at different options and capitalizing on certain strengths. What strengths do you feel you have? Are you someone who is good at building? Do you have good social skills? Ask God to help you find out what your strengths are, and then put a plan into motion!

Strategizing is important because it will help you feel you are maximizing the time you give to be generous. Most organizations will ask that you plan ahead so that they can prepare opportunities to allow you to feel the most effective with your time spent. Set up the meeting before the meeting, and ask what the need is. When we can see the need, we can meet the need. Putting the time in beforehand will stir up a greater passion in you, wherever you are serving.

"Commit to the Lord whatever you do, and he will establish your plans" (Proverbs 16:3 NIV).

## Serve

Once you have finished strategizing what and where you plan to be generous, you will have the opportunity to follow through. Serving is always best done when you are in tune with the Holy Spirit. Sometimes an immediate need comes with a decision for immediate action—a car on the side of the road or a homeless man asking for food. If we stay connected with God's spirit, we will find a greater joy and purpose in serving. During the time leading up to and while you are serving, ask the Holy Spirit how you can make yourself available in generosity to the people who are with you. Remember that serving can either encourage or exhaust you and the people you are serving, based on your attitude. People are most affected by the service done by the person who serves them in a way that expresses that there is no place that person would rather be than serving them.

"Never be lacking in zeal, but keep your spiritual fervor, serving the Lord" (Romans 12:11 NIV).

## Save

We all love to be loved; there is no doubt about that. Countless ballads have been written about the beauty of being in love and probably equally as many songs have been written of pain and anguish about missing love. Love and love that expresses God's heart for humanity is capable of transforming human life. If you have served in any capacity, you probably are aware of the phrase, "I came in thinking I would help change their lives, and instead they changed mine." A deep expression of appreciation for our simple generosity from someone in need can make for amazing moments for us. It is incredible what generosity with an attachment of love can do.

I have a file in my office that has expanded over the years with thank-you letters and notes from people to whom I've had the opportunity to be generous. Sometimes when my day doesn't go so well or I need some inspiration, I will open up that drawer and read a few of them. I am immediately brought back to the exact moment when serving happened and brought to a place of purpose and direction. You may not always receive accolades or people patting you on the back when you do something—really, we are not generous because we seek that kind of approval—but save the moments when what you did mattered. Save the thank-you notes and cards of encouragement. Create a generosity journal or a serving scrapbook, and record the moments when you felt alive in your giving. Watch that grow over time, and let it motivate you to maintain an attitude of giving. And above all else, know that in your serving you have caught the heart and attention of the Man who made you.

"Whoever brings blessing will be enriched, and one who waters will himself be watered" (Proverbs 11:25 ESV).

# 22

## Ask, Allow, Activate

If someone were to ask you right now what your favorite season is, what would you say? Some might choose autumn because all the leaves turn color, and it means that the pumpkin spice latte is back at Starbucks. Some might say spring, when it is not too hot, and it's not too cold. If you asked that question of anyone in Wisconsin, most would respond with summer. Summer is a very valuable time where I am from because we do not get enough of it. We have spring, which of course leads us into summer, and it lasts almost long enough for us as a blink, followed by a two-month autumn, and then eight months of blisteringly cold winter. I don't know what the seasons look like where you live, but keeping generosity alive in our lives sometimes feels like seasons. Maybe we are in the summertime in our lives, where things are great and we feel warm toward serving. Or maybe we are in winter, and things are not so great and we feel cold toward serving. How do we keep our generosity warm in the winter and hot in the heat? I believe when you ask, allow, and activate God and generosity in your life, you can keep the temperature of generosity warm.

## Ask

One of the phrases I hear commonly in church is, "You have not because you ask not." We, as humans, are not wired with the ability to read to each other's minds. (Thank God too because that would be awkward for all of us.) The mind of generosity cannot be read. We expect God to just barge in sometimes because He is supposed to know our hearts. He does, but remember He is also a gentleman. Asking shows a sign of humility and moves generosity from just being in your mind to being put into motion. What if we made the commitment to finding out what people needed before they had to ask us out of their desperation? We will never run short of opportunities to influence lives, but we will miss out on opportunities if we do not use the voice that God gave us to simply ask. As long as we keep asking, we will keep receiving.

"Ask, and it will be given to you; seek, and you will find; knock, and it will be opened to you" (Matthew 7:7 NIV).

## Allow

Have you ever gone on a field trip? You might have gone to the zoo to check out the animals. My personal favorite was getting free stuff at the apple orchard. Before a field trip can happen, though, you need to turn in a golden piece of paper—the permission slip. The permission slip gives all the details of the event—the date, time, and place of the activity. That piece of paper also determines your fate on whether you can go on the field trip or not. If you turn it in, you are in, and if you don't, it is a regular school day and much regret. We tend to treat God like turning in a permission slip. God wants to use us for great things, and we figure if He can give the date, time, and place for what He wants to do—and as long as it doesn't interfere with our schedule—we will sign off.

We try sometimes to live like we own the owner of our lives. The problem is that God has set up the field trip of our lives, and not allowing Him to take us on that journey leaves us sitting in the classroom while everyone else enjoys the benefits of saying yes to the journey. The best part is that God already has given us the permission to live generously—no slip needed. He isn't looking for the most talented or the best dressed. He just wants someone who is willing. It isn't limited to one date, time, or place, though, because we are not expected to have a moment but to live an experience. Instead of our allowing ourselves to say yes to God, let's live in a way that allows God to say yes to us.

"Therefore, my beloved, as you have always obeyed, so now, not only as in my presence but much more in my absence, work out your own salvation with fear and trembling, for it is God who works in you, both to will and to work for his good pleasure" (Philippians 2:12–13 NIV).

## Activate

Let me give you a little run-down as to what is going on around me at the moment. I am sitting in a coffee shop that currently has an employee talking with a customer; a coffee machine running and grinding beans; caffeine addicts sitting across the room, talking loudly, having an intervention; and a door with a bell that rings every time it opens and closes.

Those are only a few of the noises that have occurred in the last thirty seconds. Yet quite a few people in this coffee shop are spending time studying or reading books or doing other things that require concentration. I'm not sure when a coffee shop was determined to be the best place to focus, but still, I feel like I am in the zone. There are plenty of things here that could crash my focus, but I am on a mission.

Have you ever heard the phrase, "You can do anything that you set your mind to do"? There is a lot of truth in that simple statement because having a goal will often create focus for us. God wants our focus. That is why He talks about wanting to be the center of our lives and our priorities, and He wants to be our king and many other names that describe His position of focus. When you make God your priority, He will give you ability. When you give Him your ability, He will give you creativity. When you give Him creativity, He will stir you motivationally. When you are motivated, you will be activated. It all begins with setting a focus. God wants to drown out the noise of everything else and position you for one goal, and that is to point people to Him. And when you decide to activate the goal, this world has the opportunity to never be the same.

"And I am sure of this, that he who began a good work in you will bring it to completion at the day of Jesus Christ" (Philippians 1:6 NIV).

## Additional Thoughts

On a scale from 1 to 10 (1 being worst; 10 being best), where does your generosity rate?

## Ask

Simply asking moves your generosity from being in your mind and puts it into motion.

Ask the people in your circle if there is anything with which they currently need help (school, home, work).

## Allow

God will not force His hand to make you do something that you yourself will not allow Him to do.

## Activate

Creation + Motivation = Activation

What is one simple thing you could do this week to activate generosity in your life?

## Accountability

Find someone in your life who can hold you to "generosity accountability." Connect with that person throughout the week, and celebrate moments where you were able to be generous.

# 23

## The Real MVP
## (Most Valuable Provider)

One day during my senior year of high school, I was called down to the principal's office through the intercom that was in our classroom. Whenever that happened, students immediately had fear run through their veins, followed by confusion as to why they'd been called.

Luckily for me, a handful of students were all sent to the office at that time, so there was strength in numbers. Much to my surprise, when I got down there I was handed a sheet of paper that read:

> "Congratulations! Your classmates have voted you most likely to live a life of the rich and the famous."

I just laughed. Clearly, my classmates did not know me that well because I lived in a single-parent home, and I'd been called into ministry, which meant much of the riches I would get would be when I entered heaven.

When those ballots went out, my classmates somehow were convinced that I would be successful and would work hard to provide myself with a rich and famous lifestyle. I would probably have a high-profile job, a big bank account, and a sweet ride. At least, that's what my high school classmates probably thought. Look at the some of the famous figures in history. Martin Luther King Jr. spoke on behalf of his race to give them hope. Mother Teresa provided care for orphans and did missions work. Even Michael Jordan provided excitement and forever changed the game of basketball. We quantify success based on what we can provide. If that's the case, then Jesus is the most successful figure in all of history. He is that because of what He provided, making Him the real MVP—and He gave it all away to get there.

We can sometimes feel like we are the MVP, that we have worked hard to get ourselves to where we are. Like my moment of receiving my award, a little pride can set in and leave us thinking we did it all on our own, shifting our focus away from the real MVP. Pride will want to come in and slowly deceive you and prevent you from being generous. God is looking for people who will humble themselves before Him and keep their eyes on the MVP. It can be discouraging to hear that we will never out-give God, but when we remember that His Son's life was given with us in mind, God will be seen as the MVP of our lives.

# 24

## Open Doors

Remember my telling you about my ability to forget and lose things? I lost my keys fairly often, so now I have a key ring with all my keys on it. I have my house keys, office keys, and car keys, just to name a few. I know that with these keys, I will be able to open the doors to where I need to go.

In our lives, God holds the key ring for each one of us, and one of those keys is the key of generosity. God takes the key, opens the door, and then offers that we would walk through it.

My prayer for you is that you will walk through the open doors of generosity that God will set up for you, that you will see and reap the great rewards God has waiting for you as you choose to be generous, and that you will find it satisfying, filling you with joy and making you feel more alive than you have ever been.

In faith, if we stay available, aware, intentional, and sacrificial, with a heart that is bent toward God, there are no limitations to the impact and influence we can have on this world. We were created on purpose, for a purpose, and with a purpose. With each simple provision that we see and choose to meet, we can walk one step closer to a world that knows who their real provider is. With each step, we can start a "Generosity Movement."

With much love and excitement for you,
—Zach

# Verses on Generosity

**Proverbs 11:24–25**

One gives freely, yet grows all the richer; another withholds what he should give, and only suffers want. Whoever brings blessing will be enriched, and one who waters will himself be watered. (ESV)

**Proverbs 19:17**

Whoever is generous to the poor lends to the Lord, and he will repay him for his deed. (ESV)

**Matthew 6:21**

For where your treasure is, there your heart will be also. (NIV)

**Matthew 10:42**

And whoever gives one of these little ones even a cup of cold water because he is a disciple, truly, I say to you, he will by no means lose his reward. (ESV)

**Luke 6:38**

Give, and it will be given to you. Good measure, pressed down, shaken together, running over, will be put into your lap. (ESV)

**John 3:16**

For God so loved the world, that he gave his only Son, that whoever believes in him should not perish but have eternal life. (ESV)

**Acts 20:35**

In all things I have shown you that by working hard in this way we must help the weak and remember the words of the Lord Jesus, how he himself said, "It is more blessed to give than to receive." (ESV)

**2 Corinthians 9:6–7**

The point is this: whoever sows sparingly will also reap sparingly, and whoever sows bountifully will also reap bountifully. Each one must give as he has decided in his heart, not reluctantly or under compulsion, for God loves a cheerful giver. (ESV)

**Ephesians 3:20–21**

Now to him who is able to do immeasurably more than all we ask or imagine, according to his power that is at work within us, to him be glory in the church and in Christ Jesus throughout all generations, for ever and ever! Amen. (NIV)

**1 Timothy 6:18–19**

They are to do good, to be rich in good works, to be generous and ready to share, thus storing up treasure for themselves as a good foundation for the future, so that they may take hold of that which is truly life. (ESV)

**Hebrews 13:2**

Do not forget to show hospitality to strangers, for by so doing some people have shown hospitality to angels without knowing it. (NIV)

# Resources

1  http://www.oxforddictionaries.com/us/definition/american_english/
   aware
2  http://www.oxforddictionaries.com/us/definition/american_english/
   intentional
3  http://www.oxforddictionaries.com/us/definition/american_english/
   sacrificial
4  http://www.oxforddictionaries.com/us/definition/american_english/
   available

Visit and like our page at
facebook.com/GenerosityMVMNT to read stories
of generosity as well as share your own!